Remember Who
You
Are

Remember Who
You
Are

You Are Loved and Carry the
Authority of Jesus

Ken Winton

DESTINY IMAGE₍ᵣ₎ PUBLISHERS, INC.
P.O. Box 310, Shippensburg, PA 17257-0310
"Promoting Inspired Lives."

This book and all other Destiny Image, Revival Press, MercyPlace, Fresh Bread, Destiny Image Fiction, and Treasure House books are available at Christian bookstores and distributors worldwide.

For a U.S. bookstore nearest you, call 1-800-722-6774.
For more information on foreign distributors, call 717-532-3040.
Reach us on the Internet: www.destinyimage.com.

ISBN 13 TP: 978-0-7684-0283-4
ISBN 13 Ebook: 978-0-7684-8806-7

For Worldwide Distribution, Printed in the U.S.A.

1 2 3 4 5 6 7 8 / 16 15 14 13 12

Dedication

To Becky

Becky, you simply are the delight of my life. You express your commitment to us in more ways than I can count. What amazes me the most about you is you get me; what a gift you are. You are easily the greatest earthly gift God has ever given me. You truly are Jesus with skin on.

I Love you, and I am glad that with Jesus we will be together eternally.

To Kara, Paul, Joshua, Sara, Jason and Julissa

I have the great pleasure of being your Dad. You have brought me immense joy; and you have also stood by me, even in my most difficult hours.

It gives me delight to watch each of you and your families reach for God. God has delighted you with amazing spouses and kids! So, remember who He says you are and all will be well.

To The Prayer House in Chico CA

The lovers of God at The Prayer House have been intense and passionate about the spirit of intercession and worship. Their dedication to stay on the wall of intercessory worship is inspiring to others and myself. They never quit and God is noticing.

You know that the impact of your spiritual intimacy with God means every thing to the kingdom of God. It has and always will be my pleasure to grow with you in our fascination of Jesus. I admire each of you and, more importantly, our heavenly Father admires you and yes, He likes you!

Acknowledgments

Many individuals have poured into me through the years and there is no way I could begin to thank everyone who has invested in me. Your Godly DNA and collective knowledge has moved me closer and closer to the King and comes out within this book. Thank you for your personal counsel and advice. You have spoken into me at just the right season. I am eternally grateful and I am continuing the discipleship by pouring into others.

I will never forget Walt. I want to acknowledge you and thank you for being just like Jesus. When I was completely and utterly lost, you introduced me to my Savior, Jesus.

Pastor Phil Ensley is and has been one of my closest friends. I remember all the questions I had as a new believer and you were always there with help and encouragement. Therefore I acknowledge your powerful influence in my life. Thank you!

Pastor Chris Reyes is a man who has received me and pushed me into the loving arms of my heavenly Father. You have given me immense counsel, and you have always believed in me. You are more to me than my Pastor. You have been a phenomenal leader and friend to me. Thank you!

Dave Johnson and Jeff VanVonderen. You have had a massive effect on my relationship with our eternal Father. Your wealth of kingdom insights has catapulted me deeper and deeper into a revelation of Jesus. I have used your materials for years and I thank you for your important writings and teachings on the bridal paradigm.

To Christina Files. Your input and creative editing on this book have been brilliant. Along with being a professional editor you have become a good friend. Thank you.

Endorsements

Ken is a dear friend of mine. Not only as the director of The Prayer House in Chico California, but truly as a man of prayer. I know Ken has written this book from the place of deep intimacy, with a steady gaze on Jesus, his eternal bridegroom. I believe "Remember Who You Are" will be a great resource, and open the minds of those who read it. Ken so clearly lays out who we are in Christ 'now' and shows us how we can live confidently in the affections of a passionate bridegroom-God, whose love is unmoved by our weaknesses.

EDDIE BOASSO
Senior Leadership at the International House of Prayer in Kansas City

Ken's journey has given him much to teach, and that he does in a marvelous way. His book covers so many vital areas of theology, experience and passion for Jesus. Whether someone is new to Jesus or a seasoned veteran, it is a truly great read.

FRANCIS ANFUSO
Senior Pastor, The Rock of Roseville and Conference Speaker

It is a privilege for us the bride of Christ to know God's desire to keep giving himself to us in amazing and transforming ways. God has given Ken a deep insight of truth for our generation. A deep awakening is what this book will do to every reader. In light of the hour we live, Remember Who You Are is a must read by Christ's bride. I believe this book will do as much for this generation of believers as the American Revival of 1905 did for that generation.

MIKE KINGSLEY
CEO and President of Latter Glory World Mission and Only Prayer America

"Remember Who You Are" is a wonderful exclamation of the Father heart of God and a bold exhortation to every believer to know and rely on the love God has for us! Ken's insight and instruction challenged my thinking and understanding of Grace, walking in the Spirit, and being the Bride of Christ. Throughout the book and into your daily life you will hear the Spirit saying my child... "Remember Who You Are"!

BONNIE REIMERS
International Conference Speaker

Ken will knock you off the couch of your comfortable beliefs. You may think he has overstepped some boundary. I just challenge you to examine his arguments. Ken is my very dear friend of multiple decades and has always been a uniquely engaging person, but the path on which God has led him has singularly equipped him to be the champion of grace he is today. You may discover the boundaries of God's love and mercies are broader than you ever imagined!

PHILIP ENSLEY
Pastor, First Southern Baptist Church
Reedley, CA
Hospice Chaplain

Contents

Introduction

*I was receiving a revelation of Jesus and my life
was about to change.*

I n the early 1980s my wife and I took our kids to our annual "family camp" at Alliance Redwoods Conference Grounds nestled in the serene mountains just east of the Pacific Ocean and north of San Francisco, California. The first year, Pastor (and now friend) Dave Johnson from Open Door Community Church in Minneapolis, Minnesota was the speaker. Throughout the week, Dave spoke from the book of Matthew, specifically Chapters 4 and 5.

> *Jesus went throughout Galilee, teaching in their synagogues, preaching the good news of the kingdom, and healing every disease and sickness among the people. News about him spread all over Syria, and people brought to him all who were ill with various diseases, those suffering severe pain, the demon-possessed, those having seizures, and the paralyzed, and he healed them. Large crowds from Galilee, the Decapolis, Jerusalem, Judea and the region across the Jordan followed him* (Matthew 4:23-25 NIV).

Jesus was performing miracles and He healed everyone the people brought to Him. Jesus healed paralytics, demoniacs, the blind, the sick, and those with deep emotional scars. Starting in Galilee, thousands jumped on the bandwagon and began to follow Jesus because He was moving in the fullness of the kingdom of God.

From Matthew Chapter 5, Dave further taught that the kingdom of God is real today and that Jesus preached both good and bad news. The good news is that the miracles of the kingdom of God are very much real and accessible to all believers today. The bad news is that the kingdom of God is not going to flow to and through whom you think it will. Many Christians assume that the kingdom of God will only flow through religious leaders and those that look real shiny on the outside. But, Jesus described what a kingdom person looks like and what they desire. Jesus said that the kingdom of God and its power would move through people who are broken, mourning, and hungering and thirsting for righteousness.

I was becoming aware of my own brokenness. I was beginning to understand that "the poor in spirit" meant that I was spiritually bankrupt. I had nothing that I could offer to God but yet I was inheriting the kingdom of God. I was so hungry and so thirsty for God and His righteousness. I was beginning to be satisfied by the Holy Spirit. I kept asking God to give me wisdom and revelation so that I could know His Son better. My spiritual eyes were beginning to be opened by God's love. I was starting to see the hope of Jesus' calling on my life.

My family and I traveled to family camp for three summers and listened to Dave Johnson and one of his associates, Jeff Van-Vonderen, teach about the kingdom of God and our identity in Christ through the bridal paradigm. Their teaching served as a catalyst that caused me to re-examine everything I believed about sin, the flesh, sanctification, and even my salvation. The Holy Spirit was invading my soul with this life-changing message.

The Journey Continued

Three years into this voyage of understanding more about the kingdom of God, I was asked to pastor a church that had a rough history. Alongside others, I co-labored in helping this church through a process of reformation. I was so excited to teach others the fresh revelation God had been giving me concerning grace and who we are in Christ. As I began to teach, there was such an outpouring of salvation. The church went from 30 people to over 200 in a short period of time, and most of them were brand-new believers. To say the least, we were overwhelmed at this move of God.

I taught this message of identity for some time until some of the leaders in the church became discontented with my teaching and wanted to meet with me. In hindsight, I realize that I did not fully understand the subject matter that I was teaching. I knew that I was preaching the truth, but I was unable to effectively share apologetics for my message about who God says we are to Him. Consequently, I was asked to step down from my position as pastor.

To say I was devastated would be a serious understatement. I collapsed emotionally, spiritually, and physically. I was too immature in my own identity to handle the rejection that I felt from the church leadership. To me, being fired from a ministry position was the worst of failures. I could not separate my inability to effectively teach the subject of identity from who I was. I had reached the bottom of life. I remember being so afraid. For the first time in my life, I contemplated suicide. I felt all the pain of being abandoned. All my sense of worth and value as a spiritual leader exited. I did not realize it at the time, but I was finding all of my success wrapped up in what people thought of me as a pastor.

Ironically, the very topic I was teaching on was what I needed to hear and respond to. As I was teaching, God was using the bridal paradigm message to free me from my own cycle of performance for love. I was on the journey of discovering who I was to God. God was out to reveal Himself to me and was committed to letting me know who I am to Him.

Shortly after being fired, I was lying in my bed and, in the midst of all my emotional and spiritual pain, my friend, Pastor Terry Wardle, came to see me.

Terry spoke a prophetic word into my spirit:

> "Ken, you have taught the truth of who we are to God, but sadly you have only revealed 10 percent of the iceberg. Are you aware that only 10 percent of an iceberg is revealed to the naked eye? The depth of the iceberg (90 percent of it) is under the water. But God says, 'While you have heard the truth of who you are to me, I am now going to allow you to experience who I say you are. And you will teach the other 90 percent (of the bridal paradigm message) to many people throughout the world because I am beginning to release the message of identity to my bride. The bride will know her Bridegroom, Jesus."

Terry was speaking God's heart to me. Through much tribulation, trials, joy, and excitement, as well as 20 years of growing in my own identity as His child, I have had the great pleasure of training and teaching others throughout the earth about who God says we are to Him. I consider it a privilege to be called His beloved. He has truly brought me (and you) from death into life through salvation by the blood of His only Son, Jesus. We are reconciled to God to experience life abundantly.

The Spirit and the bride say, "Come!" And let the one who hears say, "Come!" Let the one who is thirsty come; and let the one who wishes take the free gift of the water of life (Revelation 22:17 NIV).

This verse is one of the most informative and significant prophecies in the Bible describing the end-times Church. John describes what will happen in the Church in the generation that the Lord returns.

This prophecy describes the Church in deep unity with the Holy Spirit. The Bride of Christ is saying and doing what the Holy Spirit is saying and doing. The Spirit is interceding for Jesus to come to His Church. The Spirit is revealing the Church's bridal identity (who we are as Jesus' Bride). In other words, the Word of God tells us what the Spirit of God will emphasize in the end times.

For the *first time* in history, just prior to the return of Jesus, the worldwide Church will be in dynamic unity with the Spirit, and the Spirit will be resting on and moving through the Church in great power. The Holy Spirit will universally emphasize the Church's spiritual identity as Jesus' Bride. Notice that John does not proclaim that the Spirit and the *family* say, "Come," nor the Spirit and the *army*, the *kingdom*, the *body*, the *temple*, or the *priesthood*. Rather, it is the Spirit resting on the Church as a bride. The beauty of this reality is that the Bride will function as the family of God, an army, the kingdom of God, the body of Christ, and the Bride moving in her priesthood.

We must know who we are to God. He is preparing His Bride for extravagant and powerful encounters with Him. These encounters will launch His Church into boldness and heavenly power (see Acts 4:29-32).

Why Read This Book On Bridal Paradigm?

Despite all of our commitment, many of us are still apathetic instead of jubilant over who God says we are to Him. Maybe there is a reason why the Church is so sleepy to this reality? Maybe we misunderstand what God says about us? Maybe we are frustrated with typical teachings from the Bible and are not willing to discuss our dissatisfactions? Maybe it has been implied that we are to be consumed with rededicating, recommitting, or to trying to be different? I will tackle these sluggish professions of faith concerning the flesh, the soul, and our brand-new spirit.

I realize that some of my teachings are against the grain and therefore you may be challenged by some of my writings. I believe you will learn some things from this book, but equal to that, I hope you unlearn some things as well. My hope is that you are challenged enough to continue reading. I trust you will be provoked internally to investigate what the Word of God says about who you are to Him.

The great eternal exchange has occurred through salvation and we have been embraced with an outrageous authenticity of an exchanged life, His for ours. God's heart is exploding with desire for each of us and He will not relent until He has all of us.

It is from this position that I release this book. I am convinced that this message will change your life, because it has changed my life as well as the lives of many others. I pray that God will intensify the revelation of Jesus into your soul. May you step into the kingdom movement of God, and may you increase your activity through recognizing the authority that you now have as the Bride of Christ!

Chapter 1

The True Nature
of God

It is time to meet the true God and to know His
nature and character.

My wife is a clinical psychologist and is the director of a local counseling center and foster care agency. Becky could tell you horrific and sad stories about some of the children her agency has ministered to in the past. Some of these kids have had anything but an emotionally healthy environment to grow up in. Most have been infiltrated with lies and shaming messages designed to control and manipulate them. In some of these children, the shame grid has been well formed.

I also encounter a lot of people who come from shame-based families who do not recognize that their real problem is shame and a sense of defectiveness. They cope and find fulfillment by manipulating their own behavior and the external circumstances around them.

Many people have lived in exhausting and emotionally shaming households. Some have experienced physical and sexual abuse by their family members or caregivers. Many have grown up with absentee parents or parents who made statements like "Children are to be seen and not heard." Some people have grown up in triangle relationships. Many people have experienced families that function in coded messages, which produce performance behaviors or encourage them to give up.

Many followers of Christ, who have suffered the travesty of shame, have attempted to find solace by studying the varied doctrines of God while missing the realness of His pure heart toward them. After years of experience, I have concluded that no matter how much doctrine a believer may know, a person will not experience deep and true victory until he or she has a true sense that God is always good and gracious.

God Is Always in a Good Mood

The *Merriam-Webster's Dictionary* defines the word *mood* as "a conscious state of mind or predominant emotion or feeling; a prevailing attitude; a disposition; a receptive state of mind predisposing to action."[1]

This definition is but a glimpse into the mood of God toward His creation. God's mood is completely objective while the human mood is often subjective and unsanctified. For example, if a person cuts me off on the road, it might make me angry and put me in a bad mood. In this case, I may have allowed another person's actions to influence my thoughts, behavior, and potential actions. God is not subject to such emotional immaturity. His emotions are always pure. He never changes.

It makes no sense that God is mad instead of glad. We make statements like, "Certainly we must do something to pay for disappointing God." That is unredeemed thinking and certainly not true. God is in a good mood, and we do not have to do anything more to get God to love us! Zephaniah tells it all.

> *The Lord your God is with you, the Mighty Warrior who saves. He will take great delight in you; in his love he will no longer rebuke you, but will rejoice over you with singing* (Zephaniah 3:17).

We need vital revelation about a joyful God!

Some will also ask, "Doesn't God send temptations to test our faith?" The Bible answers this so clearly in the book of James:

Let no one say when he is tempted, "I am being tempted by God"; for God cannot be tempted by evil, and He Himself does not tempt anyone. But each one is tempted when he is carried away and enticed by his own lust (James 1:13-14 NASB).

We keep confusing God with the enemy. God does not tempt. He always assures us that there is a way of escape from temptation (see 1 Cor. 10:13). Remember that Christ was tempted *by the devil* in the wilderness (see Luke 4:2). The book of Hebrews says, *"For since He Himself was tempted in that which He has suffered, He is able to come to the aid of those who are tempted"* (2:18 NASB). This does not say that He tempts, but rather that He comes to help those who are tempted.

God is not tempting people. He is not making people sick or diseased. God does not have an angry disposition toward humanity. In Scripture you never see Jesus laying hands on people to impart sickness to them. Instead, He healed everyone who came to Him (see Matt. 4:24; 8:16; 12:15; Mark 3:10).

Many times we quote Romans 8:28 to encourage ourselves during trying times: *"And we know that in all things God works for the good of those who love him...."* Although God makes all things work for good, He is not the author of all things. He will take what happens and use it for good, but He does not author or initiate everything that happens on this earth.

Don't believe lies about the nature of God. Look at Scripture and the life of Christ, and you will start to recognize that God is always good.

It's Time to Meet the Best Father

Even though some of us grew up in stable and functional homes, had good fathers, and are good fathers ourselves, we all need to know the *best* Father ever!

It is time to meet the true God and to know about His nature and character. I want you to clearly see the one who loves you with an everlasting love. Who is the one whose perfect love casts out all of your fears? The God who is always in a good mood!

It is okay to struggle with Him; He is a big God who can handle it. I know that God has received bad press and publicity from individuals who misrepresent Him. The true nature of God graciously volunteered His Son for you just so He could get you back. He is willing to accept you unconditionally, and He wants to partner with you.

David cries out to God while simultaneously challenging Him in this psalm:

> *My God, my God, why have you forsaken me? Why are you so far from saving me, so far from the words of my groaning? O my God, I cry out by day, but you do not answer, by night, and am not silent.* **Yet you are** *enthroned as the Holy One; you are the praise of Israel* (Psalm 22:1-3).

David was so bold with God, using statements like, *"My God, my God, why have you forsaken me?"* David was so comfortable with God's love that he knew he could be bold and challenge God. Yet every time David blared at God (because he felt safe with Him), he would conclude with praise and truth. *"**Yet you are** enthroned as the Holy One; you are the praise of Israel"* (Ps. 22:3).

Happy Are...

In Matthew 5:4, Jesus teaches, *"Blessed* [happy] *are those who mourn for they will be comforted."* We typically think that "to mourn" evokes a picture of people grieving at a funeral, wearing black, and hanging their heads down low and weeping because a loved one has just passed away. Or we think about mourning over our fallen world full of sin, mourning over the complacency of the Church, and so on.

While these are all true of mourning, I believe Jesus was referring to something even deeper in Matthew 5:4. I believe Jesus was saying: Blessed (happy) are those who get on the outside what is really going on in the inside, for they receive comfort. God makes a statement of truth. Allow me to explain. When we are real with God and we tell Him what is really going on inside our souls (mind, will, and emotions), He supernaturally brings peace and comfort. God is fully aware of the stuff that is going on inside us. He is simply waiting for us to share it with Him so that He can deliver His great comfort.

This is actually what David was doing in Psalm 22. David was telling God exactly what was going on inside of him. David began to receive comfort from God as he declared who God is: *"Yet you are enthroned as the Holy One; you are the praise of Israel"* (Ps. 22:3).

In the beatitudes, Jesus was proclaiming what believers act like and what they produce. *"Blessed are the poor in Spirit..."* (Matt. 5:3). They are spiritually bankrupt, yet they get the kingdom of God. All things in the kingdom are backwards to the things of this world. We have nothing to give God, but we get all things. Blessed are those who mourn and tell God everything that is going on in their souls for they will receive comfort from God. Kingdom people have the privilege of telling God everything because they know that He will receive them and all their frailties and weakness. He actually loves our weakness!

God's Transforming Love

God loves us in the same way that God loves Himself. The measure of the Father's love for Jesus is the measure of His love for us. This is the ultimate statement of our worth to God. This reality gives believers the right to view themselves as "God's favorite." It is not difficult to believe that God loves perfected believers in heaven. The difficulty comes with believing that He has affection for weak people in this age. God loves us like God loves God. *"As the Father loved Me, I also have loved you; abide* [live] *in My love"* (John

15:9 NKJV). *"That the world may know that You...have loved them as You have loved Me"* (John 17:23 NKJV).

Jesus spoke these verses to the apostles at the Last Supper to prepare them to recover from condemnation, confusion, and disappointment after Jesus died and some betrayed Him (see John 14–17). We are to behold or be attentive to how the Father feels about us. *"Behold what manner of love the Father has bestowed on us..."* (1 John 3:1 NKJV).

The ocean of God's love includes the pleasure of us desiring and enjoying God and being tenderized by Him. This is beautifully communicated in Ephesians as Paul prays for the church:

> *So that Christ may dwell in your hearts through faith; and that you, being rooted and grounded in love, may be able to comprehend with all the saints what is the breadth and length and height and depth, and to know the love of Christ which surpasses knowledge, that you may be filled up to all the fullness of God* (Ephesians 3:17-19 NASB).

God enjoys us even in our immaturity. He delighted in David on the day of his repentance after sixteen months of compromise in Ziklag (see 1 Sam. 27-30). *"...He delivered me because He delighted in me"* (Ps. 18:19 NKJV).

God delights in showing us mercy. He wants us to be confident in the fact that He enjoys us even when we are weak. This confidence causes us to run to Him instead of from Him. *"...He does not retain His anger forever, because He delights in mercy"* (Micah 7:18 NKJV).

We must have confidence in our access to the presence of the indwelling Spirit. The Holy Spirit is the glory that Jesus gave us that empowers us to walk in unity with God's heart. Unity with God's heart is the essence of intimacy with God.

Here is what Jesus prayed:

> *The glory which You gave Me I have given them* [indwelling Spirit], *that they may be one just as We are one, I in them, and*

You in Me; that they may be made perfect in one, and that the world may know You have sent Me, and have loved them as You have loved Me (John 17:22-23 NKJV).

We place our cold hearts in the bonfire of God's presence every time we seek Him through His Word and intercession. God is thrilled every time we simply gaze upon Him!

As we have read, we know that God is the great restorer and giver of truth. He understands that if He continues to speak His truth into us, we will begin to believe Him, and we will begin to behave in a way that is consistent with who we believe we are. We were created to respond to His truth and His love.

God's immeasurable love for you is undaunted and will prevail forever and ever. He truly is in a good mood. He definitely likes you and loves to be with you as you partner with Him to bring the King and His kingdom to wherever you are.

Before I go any further, in the next chapter I will bring some understanding to what the bridal paradigm message is and what implications it has for the Church.

Summary Questions

1. How does Merriam Webster's Dictionary define the word mood?

_____

_____

_____

_____

_____

2. Do you believe that God is always in a good mood toward you? □ Yes □ No

3. If your answer to question 2 is "yes," what do you believe God says about you? If your answer to question 2 is "no," ask the Holy Spirit to give you revelation about what God thinks of you.

_____

_____

_____

_____

_____

_____

4. Read Zephaniah 3:17 in the NIV. What do the words in Zephaniah 3:17 mean to you?

_____

_____

_____

_____

_____

5. Review pages 19-21. Read James 1:13-14 in the NASB. If the enemy of God tempts us and draws us into sin, what does God do?

_____

_____

_____

_____

_____

_____

6. Have you ever been frustrated or even angry at God? If so, explain the scenario. Use another piece of paper, if needed.

_____

_____

_____

_____

_____

_____

7. Matthew 5:4 says, "Blessed [happy] are those that _____ for they will be _____" (see pages 22-23).

8. What does it mean to you to get on the outside what is really going on in the inside?

_____

_____

_____

_____

_____

_____

9. The measure of the Father's _____ for Jesus is the same measure of His _____ for us (see page 23).

   a. "As the Father _____ Me, I have also loved _____; abide [live] in My love" (John 15:9 NKJV).

   b. "That the _____ may know that You have _____ _____ as You have _____ Me" (John 17:23 NKJV).

10. What does it mean to you to know that God enjoys you even in your weakness? Before you write your answer, review Micah 7:18 in the NKJV (see page 24).

_____

_____

_____

_____

_____

_____

11. Why is God thrilled with you every time you simply glance upon Him? (See pages 23-25.)

_____

_____

_____

_____

_____

_____

Endnote

1. *Merriam-Webster's Dictionary*, s.v. "Mood"; http:// www. merriam-webster.com/dictionary/mood (accessed February 17, 2012)

Understanding the Bridal Paradigm

From this demonstration of power, the Bride of Christ will receive boldness to preach and prophesy to the lost and hurting souls of the earth.

*B*ridal paradigm is a term used to describe the analogy of Jesus as the Bridegroom and the Church as His Bride. The bridal paradigm is to be viewed as the relationship between Jesus as the Bridegroom King and the Church (individuals and corporately) as His bridal partner. It illuminates His great desire for us and our response toward Him. This analogy is seen throughout the Bible, such as in Revelation 21:9, *"One of the seven angels who had the seven bowls full of the seven last plagues came and said to me,* **"Come, I will show you the bride, the wife of the Lamb."**

Likewise, Song of Solomon 8:6-7 says:

Set me as a seal upon your heart, as a seal upon your arm, for love is strong as death, jealousy fierce as the grave. Its flashes are flashes of fire, the very flame of the Lord. Many waters cannot quench love, neither can floods drown it. If a man offered for love all the wealth of his house, it would be utterly despised (ESV).

BRIDAL PARADIGM IS A PICTURE OF HOW JESUS FEELS ABOUT US.

God wants us to experience the "superior pleasures" of the gospel as expressed through the bridal paradigm message. He knows that we are best equipped to resist the "lesser pleasures" of sin as we experience satisfaction in intimacy with Him. In the days ahead, I believe we will increasingly experience these "superior pleasures," empowering us to extravagantly follow our Bridegroom wherever He goes.

Jesus' Emotions Toward Us

God energizes our spirits with passion for Him when we understand His devotion and commitment to us as seen in the cross. The Bridegroom message includes the revelation of Jesus' emotions for us. Let's take a look at some of Jesus' emotions toward His Church.

1. Jesus the Bridegroom is filled with tender mercy.

He is gentle with our weakness. While we often confuse rebellion with immaturity, God does not. God is angry at rebellion, but He has a heart of tenderness toward sincere believers who seek to obey Him. He enjoys us even in our weakness (see Ps. 18:19,35; 130:3-4). He knows that, in our sin and weakness, His tenderness makes us run to Him instead of away from Him.

2. Jesus the Bridegroom has a thrilled and happy heart.

While on earth, Jesus had more gladness than any person in history (see Heb. 1:9). Most believers throughout Church history have thought that God is angry or sad the majority of the time when He relates to us. However, Jesus is very glad when He relates to us, even in our weakness. In Isaiah 62:4, God tells us that His Church is His *Hephzibah*.[1]

> *...But you will be called Hephzibah...for the Lord will take delight in you...* (Isaiah 62:4).

This Hebrew word translates to "my delight is in her." God is always thrilled with us! He is always bragging about us to all of heaven. God has the amazing ability to see us as the finished Bride. That's each one of us! He is fully aware of our failures, shortcomings, and sin. But this is not His focus. His focus is our righteousness and wholeness in the blood of Christ. Therefore, God is always happy with us!

3. Jesus the Bridegroom has fiery affections.

He has a burning desire and longing for His people. We are Jesus' great reward. He looks at us, His created ones, with fiery eyes of passion. Because of this great reality, we are drawn to His fiery affections.

> *As the Father loved Me, I also have loved you; abide in My love* (John 15:9 NKJV).

4. Jesus the Bridegroom is zealous.

He destroys all that hinders love (see Prov. 6:34; Zech. 1:14; 8:2; Ezek. 38:18-19; Rev. 19:2).

> *Then the angel who was speaking to me said, "Proclaim this word: This is what the LORD Almighty says: 'I am very jealous for Jerusalem and Zion'"* (Zechariah 1:14).

5. Jesus the Bridegroom possesses indescribable beauty.

He fascinates our hearts. He becomes all that we desire. He causes us to gaze on His beauty. He draws us to meditate on Him all of our days.

One thing have I asked of the Lord...to gaze upon the beauty of the Lord (Psalm 27:4 ESV).

At its core, the bridal paradigm is John 3:16: *"For God **so loved** the world that **He gave** His only begotten Son..."* (NKJV).

Jesus is overwhelmed emotionally when we look upon Him. His heart is ravished by just one look from us (see Song of Sol. 4:9). Even when we were dead in our trespasses, He made us alive together with Christ, and it is by grace we have been saved. We need to study the emotions of God.

The word *paradigm* describes a pattern upon which we arrive at a decision. Our paradigms color every experience we encounter in life. In other words, what we think, what we feel, and what we express are derived from a paradigm.

The bridal paradigm also illuminates how we feel toward Him. There is great fruit when we declare who He is and how much He delights in us.

Father, I want those you have given me to be with me where I am, and to see my glory, the glory you have given me because you loved me before the creation of the world (John 17:24).

But because of his great love for us, God, who is rich in mercy, made us alive with Christ even when we were dead in transgressions—it is by grace you have been saved (Ephesians 2:4-5).

...He delivered me because He delighted in me (Psalm 18:19 NKJV).

Place me like a seal over your heart, like a seal on your arm; for love is as strong as death, its jealousy unyielding as the grave. It burns like blazing fire, like a mighty flame (Song of Solomon 8:6).

Behold, you are fair, my love; behold, you are fair! (Song of Solomon 1:15 NKJV)

The bridal paradigm is a picture of how Jesus feels about us. The bridal paradigm is one way to tell the glorious story of how we as human beings were created by an all-sovereign, all-powerful, and all-wise God. We were established in the beautiful Garden of Eden to be in constant and eternal relationship with our Creator. He owes us nothing and needs nothing from us. Yet, out of His great compassion and love, God freed us from the law of sin and death so that we could be with Him in eternity, unto His glory.

HIS HEART IS RAVISHED BY JUST ONE LOOK FROM OUR DOVE EYES.

He freed us because He loved us. He freed us because He greatly desired us. He is not only coming back as a King to reign, a Judge to bring justice and right wrongs, but also as a Bridegroom to reveal His great love and kindness (see Eph. 2:7). It is the story of how He died for our sins, how He needed to conquer death by rising from the grave, how He went to prepare a place for us (see John 14:3), and when He is coming back for us (see Rev. 19:6-8). We are His glory (see John 17:10), and in us He has wealth and riches (see Eph. 1:18).

What the Bridal Paradigm Is Not

The bridal paradigm is not about men getting in touch with their feminine side. Men, you don't have to imagine yourself dressed in a beautiful wedding gown, holding hands with your Bridegroom Jesus, walking through the flowery meadows. We do not have to imagine ourselves kissing Jesus on the lips. Song of Solomon 1:2, *"Let him kiss me with the kisses of his mouth…,"* is not about literally kissing Jesus on His lips. It is an analogy, and the mouth represents His Word or His thoughts about us as His Bride, and the kiss represents the passionate impact His words have on our hearts. When the Bride intercedes for the kisses of His mouth, it is a request to the Father that our hearts would be impacted and set on fire by the words of Jesus so that we would love Him more.

Two Moves

God is so active in His recapturing of creation unto Himself. He postures Himself at all times to be proactive toward His pursuit of us. In other words, God will not relent until He has all of us.

Because of this, I believe there are two significant moves of the Holy Spirit occurring at this time in history. I do not mean to imply that God is limited by these two moves of the Holy Spirit, nor are these two movements the only releases coming out of heaven. Many people in the circles that I move in have observed these two activities of heaven increasing. I have also seen the Church at large beginning to advance in these two areas, and this brings evidence that God is releasing these two areas at this time in history.

First, the bridal paradigm message is being released from the hallways of heaven. Although God calls us many things, our identity as His Bride shines light on how to step out of unhealthy cycles of shame, fear, doubt, and insecurity. God is preparing His Bride for the days ahead. She must know who she is so the Church will be prepared to endure and to walk in power, demonstrating signs, wonders, and miracles. By demonstrating power, the Bride of Christ will receive boldness to preach and prophesy to the lost and hurting souls of the earth, as stated in Acts.

> *Now, Lord, consider their threats and enable your servants to speak your word with great boldness. Stretch out your hand to heal and perform miraculous signs and wonders through the name of your holy servant Jesus. After they prayed, the place where they were meeting was shaken. And they were all filled with the Holy Spirit and spoke the word of God boldly* (Acts 4:29-31).

Second, God is releasing a spirit of intercession and worship (intercessory worship) that is preparing us for the days ahead. God made a powerful promise in Isaiah that He would bring a great joy of intercession in the last days, shortly before the return of Christ. God is going to bring great joy to His house of prayer because the Bride of Christ lacks joy regarding prayer and intercession.

THE BRIDAL PARADIGM AND INTERCESSORY WORSHIP ARE INSEPARABLE AND ARE BEING RELEASED FROM GOD'S THRONE.

And foreigners who bind themselves to the Lord to serve him, to love the name of the Lord, and to worship him, all who keep the Sabbath without desecrating it and who hold fast to my covenant—these I will bring to my holy mountain and give them joy in my house of prayer. Their burnt offerings and sacrifices will be accepted on my altar; for my house will be called a house of prayer for all nations (Isaiah 56:6-7).

We must remember that intercession coming from the Bride of Christ, in agreement with Jesus (who is the Chief Intercessor), is the very fuel that will empower and release preachers and prophets to perform signs and wonders in the streets, in homes, and in the marketplace. Before the return of Christ, He will bring His Bride into deep and joyful intercession. Both of these considerable moves of God—the bridal paradigm and intercessory worship—are inseparable and are being released from God's throne. We will experience more revelation and the release of the power of heaven as we step into deep intercessory worship. I am convinced that one of the significant reasons the Church is not interceding is because she simply does not know who she is. But she will!

The Beginning and the End

Humanity's walk on earth began in a wedding where God the Father confirmed the marriage of Adam and Eve. It will culminate in a wedding where God the Father presents the Church to His Son as His Bride at the marriage supper of the Lamb. Among others, believers in Jesus have three primary identities throughout the New Testament:

1. The body of Christ

2. The sons of God

3. The Bride

But in the end, on that glorious day when Jesus returns, He is returning for His Bride, and it will be in that hour that the Bride, in full agreement with the Holy Spirit, will cry out to her Bridegroom Jesus, *"Come, Lord Jesus, Come"* (see Rev. 22:17).

This is not to diminish the importance or significance of any of the other positions we hold in Jesus. This is simply a way to view the whole of Scripture through a focused lens. When we begin to view Jesus as our Bridegroom, as the lover of our souls, as the one whose heart is ravished when He looks upon us, it moves our hearts in new ways as we begin to understand that we can only truly love Him because He loved us first. We are wooed into that place of being a lovesick Bride who only has *dove eyes* for her Beloved (see Song of Sol. 1:15).

Created to Carry Out God's Redemption

We need to go back to the beginning to see God's original purpose and desire for creation, specifically in the creation of humanity. When we recognize the pattern God established in creation, it illuminates why God chooses the allegory of marriage to relate to us. Genesis chapter 1 gives a pattern to creation. The pattern is "according to its kind."

Then God said, "Let the land produce vegetation: seed-bearing plants and trees on the land that bear fruit with seed in it, according to their various kinds." And it was so. The land produced vegetation: plants bearing seed according to their kinds and trees bearing fruit with seed in it according to their kinds. And God saw that it was good.

...So God created the great creatures of the sea and every living and moving thing with which the water teems, according to their kinds, and every winged bird according to its kind. And God saw that it was good. God blessed them and said, "Be fruitful and increase in number and fill the water in the seas, and let the birds increase on the earth."

...And God said, "Let the land produce living creatures according to their kinds: livestock, creatures that move along the ground, and wild animals, each according to its kind." And it was so. God made the wild animals according to their kinds, the livestock according to their kinds, and all the creatures that move along the ground according to their kinds. And God saw that it was good (Genesis 1:11-12, 21-22, 24-25).

The Genesis chapter 1 blueprint of creation established and brought together everything "according to its kind." God created everything to have a counterpart, including plants like grass, herbs, and fruit trees; every living thing in the waters, like sea creatures; and all living creatures. God clearly established the divine blueprint of creation. God created an original and then a counterpart "according to its kind" ten times. Why? God designed creation so that it would take two to generate life. God's purpose in union was to generate life.

Then God created people to have and take dominion over the earth.

Then God said, "Let Us make man in Our image, according to Our likeness; let them have dominion over the fish of the sea, over the birds of the air, and over the cattle, over all the earth and over every creeping thing that creeps on the earth." So God created man in His own image; in the image of God He created him; male and female He created them. Then God blessed them, and God said to them, "Be fruitful and multiply; fill the earth and subdue it; have dominion over the fish of the sea, over the birds of the air, and over every living thing that moves on the earth" (Genesis 1:26-28 NKJV).

The Uncreated One declared a most amazing statement. He created a being in His image who would have all dominion over creation. God imparts and gives dominion to those made in His image to serve as His representatives on the earth.

After God created ten consecutive times, an original and then a counterpart according to its kind or in its likeness, He did something different. In His eleventh act of creating, He didn't create an original, but instead created one in the likeness of another. The Uncreated One created us (humanity) in His likeness and image.

What was God doing? He was creating a new order of beings (humans) who were to be the counterpart of the pre-existent Uncreated One, the second person of the Trinity, Jesus. The counterpart, Adam, was created for union with Jesus, the original.

God Himself has union with a part of creation, a union that generates the flow of heavenly life through the rest of the created order. The Eternal and Uncreated One created humans for the purpose of union and intimacy with Him. The human spirit was designed in God's likeness and image. The very design of the human spirit is God's statement of His desire for intimacy. Since we were created to be in God's likeness, we are internally and eternally designed to fellowship and govern with God.

God has drawn each of us into a great and eternal partnership to engulf the earth with the beauty, power, and holiness of our Father. God chooses to recapture the earth and all of creation with His loving hands. He chooses to use us, His beloved, to assist Him in capturing the hearts of those in our generation. The reason we were born again was not to simply avoid hell, but we were born again to be a dwelling place for the one who loves us eternally. In this, we will stand with Him in the recapturing of the earth and His creation.

Humanity was created with the capacity to reign over all. God gave dominion to us as an expression of His favor and love. God had plans of royalty, of honor, of great favor for humanity. We need this kind of favor from God if we are to carry out our purpose.

The Bridal Message Invites All

In the same way that all believers are the sons of God, so are all believers the Bride of Christ. The bridal paradigm invites us all, male and female, into a relationship with our God that is based on intimacy of the heart. We are invited to become lovers of Jesus. By growing in this love, we begin to press in to understanding the length, width, height, and depth of His love for us (see Eph. 3:16-19). As we become more focused on Jesus as our Bridegroom, we are stirred into asking our Father to give us more wisdom and revelation into the knowledge of the one we love, Jesus (see Eph. 1:16-19).

This approach to God draws us into a place where, in response to His love, we long to put first what Jesus called the first and greatest commandment, to love God with extreme passion and with our whole hearts.

> "Love the Lord your God with all your heart and with all your soul and with all your mind." This is the first and greatest commandment. And the second is like it, "love your neighbor as yourself" (Matthew 22:37-39).

We embrace the Father's true love, and from this place, we can truly walk out the fruit of the new commandment of Jesus to love one another. When we truly adore God our Father, when we truly are fascinated with Jesus, and when we are captivated with the Holy Spirit, we then become motivated to love one another.

When the reality of loving one another is flowing, then we begin to understand the commanded blessing of Psalm 133.

> *How good and pleasant it is when brothers live together in unity! It is like precious oil poured on the head, running down on the beard, running down on Aaron's beard, down upon the collar of his robes. It is as if the dew of Hermon were falling on Mount Zion. For there the Lord bestows his blessing, even life forevermore* (Psalm 133).

God is willing and excited to pour out the oil of the Holy Spirit on us, and He is capable and desirous to give us the dew of refreshing. This is why God commands His blessings toward those who are first wholly devoted to Him and who love one another. We simply cannot love one another without first receiving His love. As we declare His perfect love, we will love one another and enjoy the oil of His Spirit.

Why Is God Pouring Out This Message?

First, it's important to know that we are the Bride and that He is the Bridegroom because it is biblical truth. Though it is not the gospel, it is part of it. It gives us the big picture of why God sent His Son to die for our sins—because of His love for us. It's the reason His Son, Jesus the Christ, has given us life and is coming back to the earth.

He passionately desires to reveal His great love and kindness to us. God's eternal purpose for His creation is to provide a family for Himself and an equally yoked Bride for His Son as His eternal companion who will reign with Him in love. God is rising up a prepared Bride for His worthy Son.

Second, many believe that we are living in the age in which the Lord will return. In the age when the Lord returns, it is imperative that the Bride makes herself ready (see Rev. 19:7) and that she buys oil (see Matt. 25:1-12). Matthew says that in the final days, *"because of the increase of wickedness, the love of most will grow cold, but the one who stands firm to the end will be saved"* (Matt. 24:12-13). I will elaborate more on this subject later.

Mike Bickle, director of the International House of Prayer (IHOP), Kansas City, gave a prophetic word to this generation while ministering in Cairo, Egypt. He said, *"God is going to change the understanding and expression of Christianity in one generation."* This expression isn't being changed to something new. The Church in our day is preaching many other things outside of Christianity, and God is going to bring our understanding of the good news back to the foundation of His Word.

I believe that the generation that Mike Bickle has spoken of will immediately realize that they cannot fight the battle over lost souls from the view of the pews. They will come to recognize that they need to move out into the enemy's camp. They will understand that a confined Church loses validity (relevance and meaning), that a confined Church is an expiring Church instead of an explosive Church, as it should be. I believe that this fresh generation of young believers will not allow themselves to stay in their comfort zones. They will recognize and even know instinctively that the anointing comes to people who are willing to step out of their comfort zones and proclaim who God says they are!

The bridal paradigm is not for the purpose of saying that we just found a new way to walk out Christianity. The bridal paradigm is the Bible's way of helping us understand our purpose for living and existing. God's desire has always been for us to know who we are and why we were created. When this revelation occurs in each of us, we will move in the genuine authority that we have!

In his book *Bridal Intercession*, Gary Wiens answers why God is pouring out this message.

> The whole reason we were chosen from the beginning of time was so that the passionate heart of Jesus would be satisfied! We were redeemed and adopted for a purpose, and that purpose was that Jesus might

present us to Himself as His perfect counterpart, washed in His blood, filled with glorious beauty and made fully like Him. We were created and redeemed for romance, and because of that fact, we now have the hope that our deepest longings for intimacy and significance will be satisfied through relationship with Jesus.

The fire that has burned in the heart of God since the beginning of the beginning is the passion to have a partner for His Son! We were chosen to be holy and blameless in Christ before the worlds were made, so that we might become a bride suitable for Him, a partner who is like Him. The good pleasure of the will of God the Father was to have this kind of relationship with human beings, that He might nurture us with perfect love and prepare us to be joined to His Son Jesus in the romance of the ages.[2]

The bridal paradigm message changes the way evangelists preach salvation, the way pastors counsel people through life, the way teachers explain the Bible, the way forerunners prophesy, the way entrepreneurs run businesses, and the way intercessors pray (see 1 Cor. 1:9).

In the next few chapters, we will chase down roadblocks to experiencing God. One of the greatest roadblocks to the body of Christ is spiritual abuse. In the next chapter, we will bring definition to spiritual abuse and the power and influence it carries.

Summary Questions

1. Two significant moves of the Holy Spirit are _____ and _____ (see pages 34-35).

2. Our identity as His Bride shows us how to step out of the unhealthy cycles of (see page 34):

   a. _____

   b. _____

   c. _____

   d. _____

3. Write a biblical definition of *intercession*. Feel free to use a Bible dictionary or other resource, if necessary.

   _____

   _____

   _____

   _____

   _____

   _____

4. Read Isaiah 56:6-7 in the NIV. What is the powerful promise God made about intercession? (See page 35.)

   _____

   _____

   _____

   _____

   _____

   _____

5. What are the three primary identities of believers that Jesus noted throughout the New Testament? (See page 36.)

   a. _____

   b. _____

   c. _____

6. Read Song of Solomon 1:15 in the NIV. What does it mean to see with dove's eyes?

_____

_____

_____

_____

_____

_____

7. In your own words, describe what the phrase *bridal paradigm* means (see page 39).

_____

_____

_____

_____

_____

_____

8. List some of the emotions Scripture indicates God has toward us (see pages 40-42). If necessary, use another sheet of paper.

_____

_____

_____

_____

_____

_____

_____

9. The bridal paradigm is the Bible's way of helping us under-stand our _____ for _____ and _____ (see page 41).

10. Why is God advancing the bridal paradigm message unlike during any other time in history?

_____

_____

Endnotes

1. Brown, Driver, Briggs, and Gesenius, *The NAS Old Testament Hebrew Lexicon,* s.v. "Chephtsiy bahh" (#2657); BibleStudyTools.com; http://www.biblestudytools.com/lexicons/hebrew/nas/chephtsiy-bahh.html (accessed February 17, 2012).

2. Gary Wiens, *Bridal Intercession* (Greenwood, MO: Oasis House, 2001).

Chapter 3

Is There Spiritual Abuse?

A hallmark of spiritual abuse is treating the person
who dares to point out a problem as the problem.

There are multiple forms of abuse, and all forms of abuse are painful. Just ask someone who has experienced physical or sexual abuse. I believe there is another kind of abuse that is equally horrific and can be one of the most devastating to experience. This abuse is well hidden and is at large in the spiritual arena. It is deep, pervasive, and very difficult to unravel. Spiritual abuse brings forth immense damage in the form of spiritual wounds.

Spiritual abuse is an irrefutable and unholy use of power, and it is the exact opposite of love. Spiritual abuse can occur when a spiritual leader uses his or her spiritual position to control or dominate another person. It often engages the feelings and thoughts of another, without regard to what will result in the other person's state of emotions or spiritual well-being. Spiritual abuse often refers to an abuser using spiritual or religious rank in taking advantage of the victim's spirituality by putting the victim in a state of unquestioning obedience to an abusive authority. Power is used to reinforce the position or needs of a leader above one who comes to the leader in need. Spiritual abuse can also occur when spirituality is used to make others live up to a spiritual standard. This promotes external spiritual performance or is used as a means of proving a person's spirituality.

When religious systems are not based on the truth, they cannot allow questions, dissent, or open discussions about issues. The person who dissents (rather than the issue raised) becomes the problem. The truth about any issue is settled and handed down from the top of the hierarchy. Questioning anything is considered a challenge to authority. In a controlling and spiritually abusive environment, leaders suppress those who want to think for themselves by explaining that they doubt God and His anointed leaders. Thus, the follower controls his own thoughts out of fear of doubting God.

Some in the Church have labeled individuals who have experienced the tragedy of spiritual abuse and who have dared to speak out about it as unloyal, unspiritual, judgmental, and even disobedient.

Illustrations of Spiritual Abuse

When John was a new believer, his spiritual leaders told him that he needed to give money to the church and that they needed to monitor his personal finances. As John communicated that he did not agree with this, he was labeled as disobedient. And eventually he and his family left the church.

Mike and Joni's experience is another example of spiritual abuse. This couple went to their senior pastor to talk about possibly leaving the church due to an unhealthy spiritual climate. As they were talking with the pastor, he told them that if they decided to leave the church the devil would haunt them and overrun their lives; therefore, they should stay at the church to avoid the attacks of the enemy. When they left the church, they were labeled as unloyal and unspiritual.

How Spiritual Abuse Operates

A "bounded-set" mentality does breed spiritual abuse. In this atmosphere, leaders communicate to their followers that in order to be accepted into their fellowship they need to do everything leaders tell them to do, speak the same way leaders speak, embrace what the leaders embrace, and avoid what the leaders avoid. If people in this type of atmosphere do not conform to these rules, they are never fully accepted into the fellowship. They may not be literally kicked out (although this may happen), but they will never occupy a place of authority themselves or carry any influence in the congregation.

Some religious arenas advocate that the needs of the people—what they think, feel, or want—do not matter, and they believe that the people are to meet the needs of the leadership. When spiritual leaders use their authority to manipulate or shame people into meeting their needs, it amounts to abuse. This is extremely wounding to the victim, and a place that God designed to be safe—a church—becomes unsafe. One of the greatest blockades to the bridal paradigm is spiritual abuse.

Spiritual Abuse in the Gospels

Spiritual abuse is certainly nothing new to the twenty-first century Church. Spiritual abuse was alive and well in Jesus' day. Perhaps the most obvious use of spiritual abuse is found in Matthew's gospel.

They tie up heavy loads and put them on men's shoulders, but they themselves are not willing to lift a finger to move them (Matthew 23:4).

It is interesting to note what Jesus says about spiritual abuse.

Come to me, all you who are weary and burdened, and I will give you rest. Take my yoke upon you and learn from me, for I

49

am gentle and humble in heart, and you will find rest for your souls. For my yoke is easy and my burden is light (Matthew 11:28-30).

The religious leaders of the day were placing weighty yokes on their followers. The word *yoke* comes from the Greek word *zugos*, and it is used in a variety of contexts. It can refer to balances or scales, such as those used by merchants or those that symbolize justice. In this context, the word *zugos* refers to a heavy crossbeam, which is a metaphor for being bound in slavery to a heavy load.[1]

Christ tells us that His yoke is *easy*. Great significance and meaning is packed into the Greek word for "easy," which is *chrestos*. This word is used to refer to something that has a good or excellent purpose or pleasant requirements.[2] Jesus says He offers something more excellent, something superior.

The Greek word *chrestos* can also refer to loving-kindness and mercy. When Christ says that His yoke is easy, He is telling us that it is suitable to bind us to His everlasting kindness and mercy. Christ's way of living is easier and less of a burden than false traditions, and it is a much lighter burden than the oppressive, extreme beliefs created by people. It is a beautiful thing to be yoked to Jesus!

Spiritual Abuse in the Epistles

Paul addressed the people of the church in Galatia, who were gloriously saved by Jesus through His grace alone. Throughout the book of Galatians, Paul cataloged the damage that religious leaders were introducing into the church in Galatia. Paul actually called this spiritual abuse "persecution" (see Gal. 4:29).

After Paul left the churches that were established in Galatia, many people followed Paul's example, but also began to spread a teaching about circumcision. In Galatians 6:13, Paul responds to this: *"Not even those who are circumcised obey the law, yet they want you to be circumcised that they may boast about your flesh."* In other words, if the church in Galatia agreed with this teaching, it would make them look good externally, but they would have a false sense of self-worth. Their sense of worth and value would be wrapped up in religious performance. This is completely opposite to the true kingdom of God.

Paul immediately wrote to the church in Galatia, addressing this very issue.

> *I am astonished that you are so quickly deserting the one who called you by the grace of Christ and are turning to a different gospel, which is really no gospel at all. Evidently some people are throwing you into confusion and are trying to pervert the gospel of Christ. But even if we or an angel from heaven should preach a gospel other than the one we preached to you, let him be eternally condemned! As we have already said, so now I say again: If anybody is preaching to you a gospel other than what you accepted, let him be eternally condemned* (Galatians 1:6-9).

My friends, there is a severe movement of spiritual abuse in the Church today—even in the American Church. I have had the opportunity to travel throughout the earth to speak, train, and teach, and I have seen that spiritual abuse is rampant in churches wherever I go.

The very nature of abuse is designed to destroy and keep individuals from enjoying life. All abuse is about manipulation and control, and sadly spiritual abuse is no different. This form of abuse certainly keeps us from the life that God has given each one of us. However, an understanding of the bridal paradigm message destroys spiritual abuse and will catapult us deep into His heart of love.

In the next chapter, we are going to depart from old religious thoughts and false understandings and explore what the real picture of the bridal paradigm message is.

Summary Questions

1. What are some indicators that spiritual abuse is occurring? List at least three (see pages 47-49).

_____

_____

_____

_____

_____

_____

2. True or False: Spiritual abuse is new to the twenty-first century Church. _____

3. Read Matthew 23:1-4 in the NIV. Who is Jesus talking about in verse 4?

_____

_____

_____

_____

_____

4. Read Matthew 11:28-30 in the NIV. How does Christ bring spiritual rest in the midst of spiritual abuse?

_____

_____

_____

_____

_____

_____

5. See page 50 and read Galatians 4:29. Why does Paul refer to spiritual abuse as "persecution" in Galatians 4:29?

_____

_____

_____

_____

_____

_____

_____

6. According to Galatians 1:6-9, why would you say that spiritual abuse is not the gospel of Jesus?

_____

_____

_____

_____

_____

_____

_____

7. What does the bridal paradigm message do to spiritual abuse? (See page 51.)

_____

_____

_____

_____

_____

_____

_____

8. What are we catapulted into by the bridal paradigm message?

_____

_____

_____

_____

_____

_____

Endnotes

1. Thayer and Smith, *The KJV New Testament Greek Lexicon*, s.v. "Zugos" (#2218); Biblestudytools.com; http://www.biblestudytools.com/lexicons/greek/kjv/zugos.html (accessed February 17, 2012).

2. *Ibid.*, s.v. "Chrestos" (#5543); BibleStudyTools.com, http://www.biblestudytools.com/lexicons/greek/kjv/chrestos.html (accessed February 17, 2012).

Chapter 4

God's Grace Is Not Difficult

Moment to moment, we need the power that grace offers us.

Sadly, many believers miss out on the power of God's grace and are not even aware of it because they have been taught, and even encouraged to *earn* God's grace, which was freely given to us. They generally live normal Christian lives, but secretly they wonder where the power of Jesus' words are: *"I have come that they may have life, and have it to the full"* (John 10:10b). They have a very difficult, if not impossible, time moving into abundant life. If they were honest, they might admit that they are bored and frustrated with their Christianity. They continue to exist—living a mundane life—feeling like the power of grace is limited to those who do not yet know Christ. Let's take a look at some of the reasons why Christians have a difficult time with God's grace.

Backwards

While some biblical texts seem to be under constant scrutiny, allowing new understandings of truth to emerge, I believe that Galatians 5:16 has been overlooked. As a result, many of us have taught this (and many other verses) based upon what we were taught, without challenging ourselves to examine Scripture from different angles and perspectives. I have concluded that many have been taught the truth of Galatians 5:16 backwards.

So I say, walk by the Spirit, and you will not gratify the desires of the flesh (Galatians 5:16).

The truth in this verse is significant to our relationship with sin and our sense of Christian identity. However, if we emphasize the second half of the verse without initially applying the first half, it can greatly affect the way we interpret and apply this truth. Paul clearly states that we are to walk (or live) by the Spirit. In other words, when we walk in the Spirit, we remember who God is and who He says we are. As a result, we will not carry out the desires of the flesh.

Many have been taught that if people do not carry out the desires of the flesh, then they will be walking by the Spirit. This produces a performance mentality that is rooted in the lie that says the goal of the Christian life is to stop sinning—meaning, once you stop sinning, you can then be filled with the Spirit. This approach has left many believers wondering, *If the goal is to quit sinning, why do I keep sinning and am rarely filled with the Spirit?* It is a travesty to interpret Galatians 5:16 backwards as it perpetuates a cycle of works rather than of grace.

There is nothing to work up or stop. We need to know the truth of what God has given us and done for us. When Christians believe that they somehow need to stop carrying out the desires of the flesh prior to being filled with the Spirit, they become frustrated and see no success. Look at these passages and see what God *has done!*

I have told you these things, so that in me you may have peace. In this world you will have trouble. But take heart! **I have over-come** *the world* (John 16:33).

I have written to you, fathers, because you know Him who has been from the beginning I have written to you, young men, because **you are strong***, and the word of God abides in you, and* **you have overcome the evil one** (1 John 2:14 NASB).

...every Spirit that does not acknowledge Jesus is not from God. This is the Spirit of the antichrist, which you have heard is coming and even now is already in the world. You, dear children, are from God and **have overcome** *them, because the one who is in you is greater than the one who is in the world* (1 John 4:3-4).

Everyone born of God overcomes the world. This is the victory that **has overcome** *the world, even our faith. Who is it that overcomes the world? Only the one who believes that Jesus is the Son of God* (1 John 5:4-5).

Note the present tense and indicative verbs: *has overcome; are strong; you have overcome.* These are actions released by God's favor and grace that *have been* given to us already. This is why we call it the "good news" of the gospel.

When Christians believe that they need to earn what God has already given them, they try to take care of their sin problem so they can walk in the Spirit. In this mindset, walking in the Spirit is the *goal* of the Christian life, not the *way* of the Christian life. Jesus freely gives us the ability to walk in the Spirit, which empowers us to stop fulfilling the desires of our flesh. If the goal of our Christian life is to walk in the Spirit, what will empower us to stop sinning? Nothing. When we forget that Jesus has already provided a way for us to walk in His Spirit, we unknowingly agree with lies that tell us we must try to stop sinning in our own strength. Stopping sin in our own strength is impossible—the Old Testament is full of examples of people trying to avoid sin and failing. Walking in the Spirit is possible through faith in Jesus, which empowers us to supernaturally stop sinning.

A Heavenly Revolution

God is sending a heavenly revolution of truth to His beloved Bride and awakening her to this truth and reality. As you begin to walk out this reality, it will revolutionize your relationship with Jesus!

We were created to remember who we are and to bring heaven to the earth. Salvation, signs and wonders, miracles, joy, peace, divine revelation into the knowledge of His Son, and many more things are fully accessible in heaven, and God is asking us to partner with Him to release these and more to the earth.

This is our one true destiny, to become God's own sons and daughters. Here is power and truth:

> *Dear friends, now we are children of God, and what we will be has not yet been made known. But we know that when he appears we shall be like him, for we shall see him as he is* (1 John 3:2).

In Romans, the Apostle Paul writes with great joy,

> *For as many as are led by the Spirit of God, these are the sons of God...the Spirit Himself bears witness with our spirit that we are children of God, and if children, then heirs—heirs of God and joint heirs with Christ...that we may also be glorified together* (Romans 8:14-17 NKJV).

God's Grace to Carry Out His Commands

Commands are true things from God, but we cannot carry them out without God's grace. We need His grace and power to carry them out.

> *Remain in me, and I will remain in you. No branch can bear fruit **by itself**; it must remain in the vine. Neither can you bear fruit unless you remain in me* (John 15:4).

> *I* [Jesus] ***will*** *sprinkle clean water on you, and you will be clean;* ***I will*** *cleanse you from all your impurities and from all*

*your idols. **I will** give you a new heart and put a new Spirit in you; **I will** remove from you your heart of stone and give you a heart of flesh. And **I will** put my Spirit in you and move **you** [that's us] **to follow my decrees** and be careful to keep my laws* (Ezekiel 36:25-27).

So Take a Pause

What does the Bible say about our brand-new relationship with an eternal Father? And conversely, what does it say about who we are not? At this point there are three things that you need to know about prior to this teaching:

1. You are going to have to use critical thinking.

2. I cannot teach this well enough for you to get it.

3. The Holy Spirit must invade your inner person (see Eph. 3:16); you must have revelation from the Holy Spirit as to who you are to your heavenly Father.

For people who feel defective and unwanted at the root of their souls, there is refreshing truth. So pause and ask the Holy Spirit to reveal to you who you are to the eternal Father. Ask God to show you how high, how deep, how wide, and how long His love is for you (see Eph. 3:16-19). Ask Him what it means when He says that your sins are forgiven as far as the east is from the west.

Summary Questions

1. Define biblical grace.

_____

_____

_____

_____

2. Since God's grace is not difficult, why do we struggle with it?

_____

_____

_____

_____

_____

_____

3. Galatians 5:16 says, "So I say, walk by the _____ and you won't fulfill the desires of the _____."

4. The true focus of Galatians 5:16 is walking by the _____.

5. According to Galatians 5:16, what will be the result of walking by the Spirit?

_____

_____

_____

_____

_____

_____

6. This is the *truth* of what God has given us and has done (see pages 56-57).

   "I have told you these things so that in me you may have _____. In this world you will have _____. But take heart! I have _____ the world" (John 16:33).

   "I have written to you, fathers, because you know Him who has been from the beginning. I have written to you, young men, because you are _____, and the word of God abides in you, and you have _____ the evil one" (1 John 2:14 NASB).

"Everyone born of God _____ the world. This is the victory that _____ _____ the world, even our faith. Who is it that _____ the world? Only he who believes that Jesus is the Son of God" (1 John 5:4-5).

7. Re-read page 59. Pray and ask the Holy Spirit to reveal to you who you are to the eternal Father. Write what He tells you.

_____

_____

_____

_____

_____

_____

8. Pray and ask the Holy Spirit to show you how high, how deep, how wide, and how long His love is for you. In your own words, write out what this means to you (see Eph. 3:16-19).

_____

_____

_____

_____

_____

9. Pray and ask the Holy Spirit what He means when He says your sins are removed as far as the east is from the west. In your own words, write out what this means to you (see Ps. 103:12).

_____

_____

_____

_____

Chapter 5

Humanity's Deepest Issue

Dead people don't need help; they need life.

When I travel and speak at Youth With A Mission (YWAM) bases, conferences, and churches, I always ask the question, "What is humanity's deepest issue?" The typical response is, "Humanity's deepest issue is sin, and sinners need to be forgiven."

My response is, "Okay, that is a deep issue, but do you think it is humankind's deepest issue?"

Then another understandable response comes, "The deepest issue people have is their need to be loved."

"Okay I like that, but is that their deepest issue?"

"I believe that humankind's deepest issue is selfishness."

Yes, that is certainly an issue many people deal with, but none of these issues are the deepest issue. Humanity's deepest issue is that they are dead and in need of life. Jesus Christ said that He came to give life. The prevailing question is, "What kind of person needs life?"

Paul states:

> *I have been crucified with Christ, it is no longer I who live; but Christ lives in me; and the life I **now live** in the flesh, **I live***

by faith in the Son of God, who loved me and gave Himself up for me (Galatians 2:20 NKJV).

Notice how frequently Paul uses the word *live*. Paul is communicating something profound, "I used to be spiritually dead, but now I am alive and living with Christ."

> ## FROM GOD'S STANDPOINT, HUMANKIND'S PROBLEM IS NOT JUST THAT THEY ARE SINNERS IN NEED OF FORGIVENESS; THEIR GREATEST PROBLEM IS THAT THEY ARE DEAD AND IN NEED OF LIFE.

Let me reiterate that sin is an issue and a severe issue at that. It is so severe that God had His Son bear all of our sins. Sin was in the way of us receiving God's love and experiencing never-ending life. So God removed sin from us so that we could have life with Him. Sin always highlights humankind's deepest issue—death, which is separation from God!

How Did We Die?

Let's take a look at Scripture and see if the Bible confirms that death is the deepest issue people face. When we read Genesis, we discover how humankind was created:

> *So God created man in his own image, in the image of God he created him; male and female he created them* (Genesis 1:27).

We were created in God's image. Now, what was God's command to Adam?

But you must not eat from the tree of the knowledge of good and evil, for when you eat of it you will surely die (Genesis 2:17).

God told Adam not to eat from the tree of the knowledge of good and evil, or he would die. So what happens to Adam?

When the woman saw that the fruit of the tree was good for food and pleasing to the eye, and also desirable for gaining wisdom, she took some and ate it. She also gave some to her husband, who was with her, and he ate it (Genesis 3:6).

Adam and Eve ate the fruit and spiritually died. Adam and Eve experienced spiritual death and separation from God. They did not experience immediate physical death because they were still physically alive, but they were no longer in perfect communion with their heavenly Father. They were now separated from God. They no longer were in complete and faultless relationship with Him.

The first temptation Adam and Eve faced in the garden was not whether to eat the forbidden fruit or not, but to question what God had said. *"Did God really say, 'You must not eat from any tree of the garden'?"* (Gen. 3:1). Once Satan got them to doubt the integrity and identity of God, it was easy to lure them into foolish actions.

When the serpent deceived Adam and convinced him to follow his advice rather than God's, humanity submitted to the enemy and gave authority over to him. Humankind lost their dominion, favor, and power from God. Satan was never given authority in the earth, but we give him authority when we agree with his lies and deceit. His only tool is to lie, and he is an expert at lying. He functions and moves in deceit. That's right; Satan is called a liar!

*You belong to your father, the devil, and you want to carry out your father's desire. He was a murderer from the beginning, not holding to the truth, for there is no truth in him. When he lies, he speaks his native language, **for he is a liar and the father of lies*** (John 8:44).

When Adam agreed with the serpent's lies, he gave him control. The influence that God had given to Adam in the beginning was no longer Adam's.

Does Spiritual Death Spread?

According to the book of Genesis, Adam had a son in his own image:

When Adam had lived 130 years, he had a son in his own likeness, in his own image; and he named him Seth (Genesis 5:3).

Seth was *not* born in the image of God as Adam had been. Because Adam was no longer receiving spiritual life from God, Adam's son Seth was now born in the image of Adam. According to Romans, sin entered the world through Adam's sin and spiritual death spread to all humanity.

Therefore, just as sin entered the world through one man, and death through sin, and in this way death came to all people, because all sinned (Romans 5:12).

How did Adam's sin affect all of humanity? Death was spread! So the only question remaining is how many people did death spread to? To the entire human race! According to Ephesians, we were born into this world in a sinful condition: *"As for you, you were **dead** in your transgressions and sins"* (Eph. 2:1).

Notice that before Adam and Eve disobeyed God, *"...they were both naked, the man and his wife, and were not ashamed"* (Gen. 2:25 NKJV). Now, after eating the forbidden fruit, they knew they were naked, and they made aprons and hid themselves from God's presence. Something had definitely happened to them, but it was not physical. While they were now mortal and their bodies were dying, this was not an immediate physical death, but rather a spiritual death (see Eph. 2:5; Col. 2:13). The change was on the inside. Yes, they did die, just as God had promised.

Not Ceasing to Exist

The biblical concept of death does not mean ceasing to exist, but rather means separation. In the Bible, physical death is the separation of the soul from the body. With the soul gone, the body ceases to function and begins to decay. Spiritual death means that a person's spirit is separated from God. With the spirit cut off from God, a person would still be able to function physically, but could no longer directly experience or commune with God.

Adam forfeited his intimacy with God the day he ate the fruit. The lack of intimacy with God is what we were born into. We were born into this world in the image of Adam, spiritually dead. And dead people don't need help; they need life. The Bible tells us that everything God made was very good (see Gen. 1:31). Sin, therefore, was not a natural part of creation, but an invasion from the outside. Meaning this, God has created the condition in the world where the ability to rebel against Him was possible. Yet, God is not responsible for that rebellion. Therefore, sin was not God's original plan. It originated with Lucifer, who was the first to rebel, and Adam and Eve choose to agree with Satan. Genesis 3:4-5 says, *"'You will not certainly die,' the serpent said to the woman. 'For God knows that when you eat from it your eyes will be opened, and you will be like God, knowing good and evil.'"* Adam and Eve thought they could achieve more than God had given them. Sadly, it had a drastic effect on the entire human race.

People fear physical death, but there is one reality that people fear or will fear more than anything else—spiritual death! Although not all humanity is aware of their spiritual death, all humans must eventually come to grips with their spiritual death. Many do not even acknowledge there is a God, much less that they are separated from Him. But God will be true to Himself and will bring this revelation to all. Everyone has come short of God's glory. Every knee will bow, and every tongue will confess that He is Lord (see Rom. 11:14).

A chief executive officer of a major corporation will have to wrestle with the reality of spiritual death; the homeless will grapple with spiritual death; the young and old, the strong and weak, must all deal with spiritual death (separation from God). No one can escape the spiritual death that has spread to the entire human race.

Adam, Where Are You?

In Genesis 3:9, God calls to Adam, *"Where are you?"* Remember this: When God asks a question, He is not looking for the answer. He is making a statement! Why would an omniscient (all-knowing) and omnipresent (able to be everywhere at the same time) God ask a question? He obviously knew where Adam was. *"Adam, where are you?"* was God's first statement of redemption toward the human race.

When God said *"Adam, where are you?"* God was revealing to Adam, "Satan lied to you; he duped you, he tricked you, and you agreed with him. You were taken from Me, and I am coming to get you back. You are My creation; I love you, and you will be Mine again!" God has been in the process of reconciling with humanity ever since Adam fell.

Misunderstanding Scripture

Always remember that if you feel discredited or shamed when you read a passage of Scripture, you have misinterpreted the verse. God never discredits or shames us. By no means does God use this form of motivation to get us to do what He wants. This would be out of His character and nature. The Bible is not about "should" and "ought too"—the Bible is about results. God comes from the inside out, never from the outside in. This is what Jesus meant when He spoke to the Pharisees in Matthew:

Woe to you, teachers of the law and Pharisees, you hypocrites! You clean the outside of the cup and dish, but inside they are full of greed and self-indulgence (Matthew 23:25).

Romans 12:1-2 is one of the most misunderstood passages in Scripture.

Therefore I urge you, brethren, by the mercies of God, to present your bodies a living and holy sacrifice, acceptable to God, which is your spiritual service of worship. And do not be conformed to this world, but be transformed by the renewing of your mind, so that you may prove what the will of God is, that which is good and acceptable and perfect (NASB).

Romans 12:1-2 was never written or intended to shame or control us. But I misinterpreted these two verses and lived in shame for decades. Let me tell you how I used to interpret the first verse of this passage.

The words *"I urge you"* made me feel like I needed to be a holy, living, acceptable sacrifice to God because I certainly was not acting this way. Paul was very anxious for me to live this way because I was not measuring up!

Every once in a while, I felt like I was a living sacrifice when I was teaching the Bible, or if I was leading worship, or if I gave money, but I never felt holy. Paul also stated that it was reasonable for me to act as a living and holy sacrifice to God. This made me feel like I could never measure up. Once again, I had blown it. Once again, the fact that I was not holy or a living sacrifice had been revealed.

So, I would try harder to be what Paul called me to be. Then, when I got really tired of that process and seeing no change, I began to give up trying to be holy and acceptable to God. I began to accept the fact that I would not act like Romans 12:1 on this earth. I decided that I would not be able to walk out this verse until I got to heaven. Until then, I chose to avoid the passage so that I would not feel guilty or ashamed. Many believers have or have had a similar interpretation of this verse.

More Misunderstandings of Romans 12:2

And do not be conformed to this world, but be transformed by the renewing of your mind, so that you may prove what the will of God is, that which is good and acceptable and perfect (Romans 12:2 NASB).

I used to interpret this verse to mean that I was not to play cards, to drink alcohol, to watch TV, or to see movies. In other words, I didn't do anything that non-believers did because I thought that God wanted me to be separated from the world! I felt like I was expected to have my mind changed into heavenly thoughts, and I certainly did not experience this. I gave up trying to be transformed. I assumed that these things would occur when I got to heaven.

I thought I was to know what the perfect and acceptable will of God was. I could never figure out His will. I was so frustrated. At that time, I could relate to what Paul said.

We know that the law is spiritual; but I am unspiritual, sold as a slave to sin. I do not understand what I do. For what I want to do I do not do, but what I hate I do (Romans 7:14-15).

Instead of feeling defeated and ashamed, my life became about avoiding Romans 12:1-2. This was my *previous* interpretation of Romans 12:1-2.

Through a New Lens

Now let's examine Romans 12:1-2 through the lens of the bridal paradigm.

Therefore I urge you, brethren, by the mercies of God, to present your bodies a living and holy sacrifice, acceptable to God, which is your spiritual service of worship. And do not be conformed to this world, but be transformed by the renewing of your mind, so that you may prove what the will of God is, that which is good and acceptable and perfect (NASB).

WE ARE ALREADY HOLY; WE ARE ALREADY A LIVING SACRIFICE.

In verse 1, "Therefore I urge you" is Paul's expression of intensity. Based on what Jesus did for us, Paul prepares us to listen very carefully. Because of the work of the cross, we now have God's grace and favor; this has enabled us to receive what we did not deserve.

A Clearer Translation

While the translators of the New International Version use the word *spiritual* in Romans 12:1 (NIV) *"for this is your spiritual act of worship,"* the King James Version Bible translates this word as "reasonable."

> *I beseech you therefore, brethren, by the mercies of God, that ye present your bodies a living sacrifice, holy, acceptable unto God, which is your **reasonable** service* (Romans 12:1 KJV).

I have noticed that many believers do not understand Romans 12:1 when the word *spiritual* is used. The word *reasonable* is far more comprehensive.

It is only reasonable and makes sense (because of the work of Christ) that we should present ourselves to Him in this fashion because this is what has become true about us! We are already holy, we are already a living sacrifice, and we are already fully acceptable to our Father. What a glorious and powerful reality. How freeing! This is a work that has been done by Jesus, and we are now brand-new creations!

Are We Holy?

I know you may have a hard time accepting that you are now holy before God, a living sacrifice, and that your holy God is always happy with you. When I teach about the bridal paradigm in conferences, I ask this question:

"Is God holy?"

Of course everyone responds, "Yes, He is holy."

I then ask, "What does *holy* mean?"

They respond typically with, "He is perfect. He hates sin. He is righteous. He is lacking in nothing."

"Okay, where does this holy God choose to reside? Where does He choose to live?"

They all respond with vigor, "He lives in each believer!"

Ah...this is true! God is holy, and since He is holy, He had to make the place He would live holy, too. The issue is not whether God can be around sin or darkness, but rather it is that darkness is dispelled the moment He shows up and is replaced with His glorious and powerful light.

God chooses to dwell in you:

> *that is the Spirit of truth, whom the world cannot receive, because it does not see Him or know Him, but you know Him* **because He abides with you and will be in you** (John 14:17 NASB).

Something supernatural happened to all believers the moment they received Christ as their Savior. We were moved from darkness to light; we became brand-new creations who are holy, righteous, and lacking in nothing. Something came into existence that never existed before.

You were dead in your trespasses, and God brought you from death into life. You have become born again (see John 3:3). You are now, and forevermore, holy.

Listen to Paul clearly state this reality: *"Therefore, if anyone is in Christ, he is a **new** creation; the old has gone, the **new** has come"* (2

Cor. 5:17). Believers are a new kind of creature in Christ; they are neither Jew nor Gentile. There are two Greek words that scholars have translated as "new" in English, *kaine* and *néos*. The word *néos* means "new in time" but *kaine* means a brand-new creation, as opposed to one that is renewed or improved over time.[1]

In Second Corinthians 5:17, the word *kaine* is used, meaning we are *now* brand-new creations. A true supernatural experience has occurred in each believer. The Holy Spirit of God has taken up residency in each believer. Thus, we have become brand-new creations.

This and following illustrations will help you understand what God has done for you and me.

Who We Were Before Christ

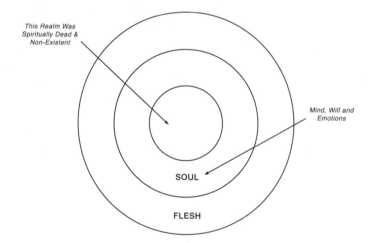

These first three circles represent us **before** we met Christ. We were created with a body and a soul. The soul realm is where our mind, will, and emotions reside. We were born without the Spirit of God resident within us. We were spiritually dead; thus, the Spirit of God in us was non-existent. We were born as sinners, separated from God, and we were prone to sin. We were enemies of God (see 1 Cor. 2:16).

But, God always delivers on His promises! In the next chapter, we will discover what God has done to bring us into life. We will realize the tremendous sacrifice God accomplished to get us back into dominion and righteousness with Himself.

Summary Questions

1. _____ is humankind's deepest issue (see page 63).

2. What brought about spiritual death? (See page 64.)

_____

_____

_____

_____

_____

_____

3. Since physical death is the separation of the _____ from the _____, what does spiritual death mean? (See page 67.)

_____

_____

_____

_____

4. Since spiritual death is separation _____ _____, what else did humankind forfeit from Satan's lies? (See page 67.)

_____

_____

_____

_____

_____

5. Read Romans 5:12. How did spiritual death enter the world and spread? (See page 66.)

_____

_____

_____

_____

_____

6. Some have felt shame about not measuring up to Romans 12:1. How have **you** historically interpreted Romans 12:1?

_____

_____

_____

_____

_____

7. According to Romans 12:1, we are already a _____ _____, _____, and _____ to God!

8. Based on the statement from #7, how do you now interpret Romans 12:1? (See pages 69-71.)

_____

_____

_____

_____

_____

9. How does it make you feel to know that God has made you a holy and new creation?

_____

_____

_____

_____

_____

_____

_____

10. What has been your understanding of Romans 12:2? You may use additional paper if needed.

_____

_____

_____

_____

_____

_____

11. According to Romans 12:2, we are not to be "_____ to this world, but to be _____ by the renewing of your _____ ...."

12. According to pages 70-71, what does it mean to not be conformed to this world?

_____

_____

_____

_____

_____

13. Why is it good to have your mind renewed?

_____

_____

_____

_____

_____

_____

14. According to Second Corinthians 5:17:
    What came into existence that never existed before?

    _____

    _____

    What has now gone away forever?

    _____

    _____

15. The three parts of the soul realm are the _____,
    _____, and _____.

Endnote

1. *Theological Dictionary of the New Testament, Volume 1,* Gerhard Kittel and Gerhard Friedrich, eds, translated by Geoffrey W. Bromiley (Grand Rapids, MI: Eerdmans Publishing Company, 1985), 388.

Chapter 6

God Makes a Promise

I will put my Spirit in you and you will live...
(Ezekiel 37:14).

What could be more frustrating than being Christians who think of themselves as self-centered sinners, yet whose purpose is to produce a life of God-centered holiness? Could this be God's intention? Have you ever wondered if God is looking at us as though we are holy, but we are really not holy? We will explore the answer to these questions in this chapter.

Can You Touch a Leper?

Before diving into God's promises, let's discuss certain truths that will reconcile any doubts we may have concerning His promises.

In the Old Testament, God was primarily revealing sin and the requirements of the Law that needed to be fulfilled. In the New Testament, God is primarily revealing His love that covers our sins and the fulfilled Law, through Jesus. In the Old Testament, if you touched a leper, you became unclean. In the New Testament, if you touch a leper, the leper becomes clean.

YOUR DOUBTS ARE NOT AS STRONG AS THE BLOOD OF JESUS.

The doubts you may have in your own mind will pin you down every time. But, your doubts are not as strong as the blood of Jesus and God's promises. The demons that continue to plague you with doubt have been vanquished to eternal hell. Even when the forces of demonic activity come down on you, let the power of God overwhelm you. It is now time to agree with God; it is a *victory* moment, not a *lie* moment. Break ranks with the lies of the evil one and come into agreement with the blood of Christ. God, through His Son, will deliver you. He promises and He never lies. He only upholds His truth, and the proof that He upholds His Word was validated when He raised His Son from the grave!

The blood of the Lamb has washed you. So let the word of your testimony come into agreement with the truth of God. Torment and shame are not part of your inheritance. It is now time to drive all demonic oppression away with God's everlasting truth. His truth was spoken from the foundations of time and lives today. There are no more accusations against you. Satan has only one tool: He lies. Everything that he delivers is a lie.

Healthy fear, such as seeing a car barreling at you and dodging out of its way because you fear being hit, is wise and normal. God gave us this emotion to protect us. This would be a good example of your emotions lining up with the truth of God.

But, when the enemy uses fear, it presents itself as a lie. Fear is nothing more than False Expectations Appearing Real. Fear from Satan is nothing more than a lie. A liar should not be believed, but the One who always tells the truth can be believed and trusted.

What Has God Promised?

Let's look at what God has promised and what He has done for us through His only Son Jesus. Here is God's phenomenal promise in Ezekiel 37:14: *"I will put My Spirit within you and you will live...."*

God has placed His Spirit in us who were dead and made us alive. We are saints who have been redeemed by the blood of the Lamb. The word *redeemed* means to set free, rescue, or ransom, to save from a state of sinfulness and all of its consequences.[1]

Consequently, the death of Christ described in Second Corinthians 5:14-15 produces a whole new order and a new mode of spiritual perception. The new order created in Christ is the new covenant (see 2 Cor. 3:6).

Remember Paul's statement in Second Corinthians 5:17: *"Therefore, if anyone is in Christ, the new creation has come: The old has gone, the new is here!"* Something has become brand-new. Something now exists that did not exist before. One can conclude from the wording in this passage that being a new creation in Christ is similar to Adam and Eve's experience prior to their fall in the paradise of Eden. It is perfect.

> *To the church of the firstborn, whose names are written in heaven. You have come to God, the Judge of all, **to the spirits of the righteous made perfect**, to Jesus the mediator of a new covenant, and to the sprinkled blood that speaks a better word than the blood of Abel* (Hebrews 12:23-24).

The real you, the born-again you, no longer sins. John carefully poses this truth to us in First John 3:9, *"No one who is born of God will continue to sin, because God's seed remains in him; he cannot go on sinning, because he has been born of God."* Everything that is true of Jesus is true of our born-again spirits (see 1 Cor. 6:17; Eph. 1:3, 15-23; Col. 2:9-10; 1 John. 4:17).

Many would back up from First John 3:9 and state that John proclaims in First John 1:8, *"If we claim to be without sin, we deceive ourselves and the truth is not in us."* Many would say, "Here is the proof that we are still sinners." But, let's bring this into full context. If we look at First John 1:1-10, we see that John, while not speaking directly to non-believers, is addressing non-believers. He is laying out what non-believers must acknowledge in order to have true fellowship with believers.

> *That which was from the beginning, which we have heard, which we have seen with our eyes, which we have looked at and our hands have touched—this we proclaim concerning the Word of life. The life appeared; we have seen it and testify to it, and we proclaim to you the eternal life, which was with the Father and has appeared to us. We proclaim to you what we have seen and heard, so that you also may have fellowship with us. And our fellowship is with the Father and with his Son, Jesus Christ. We write this to make our joy complete. This is the message we have heard from him and declare to you: God is light; in him there is no darkness at all. If we claim to have fellowship with him yet walk in the darkness, we lie and do not live by the truth. But if we walk in the light, as he is in the light, we have fellowship with one another, and the blood of Jesus, his Son, purifies us from all sin. If we claim to be without sin, we deceive ourselves and the truth is not in us. If we confess our sins, he is faithful and just and will forgive us our sins and purify us from all unrighteousness. If we claim we have not sinned, we make him out to be a liar and his word is not in us* (1 John 1:1-10).

In First John 1:10, John is speaking about non-believers. He is proclaiming that they must acknowledge that they have sinned and run to the forgiveness that Jesus offers.

Friend, You Are Free and Forgiven

As a born-again believer, your spiritual salvation is complete. At salvation, you receive the same spirit that you will have throughout all eternity. It will not have to be changed again or cleansed again.

Now if we died with Christ, we believe that we will also live with him. For we know that since Christ was raised from the dead, he cannot die again; death no longer has mastery over him. The death he died, he died to sin once for all; but the life he lives, he lives to God (Romans 6:8-10).

It has been sealed with the Holy Spirit (see Eph. 1:13) and is, therefore, sanctified and perfected forever (see Heb. 10:10,14; 12:23). Friend, you are forgiven! There is nothing anybody can do to change that! When the enemy brings up a sin from the past, he is bringing something up that is non-existent.

The rest of the Christian life is *not* about trying to obtain faith or joy or love or anything else from God, it is rather a release into our souls and bodies of what we already have in our spirits.

But the fruit of the Spirit is love, joy, peace, patience, kindness, goodness, faithfulness, gentleness and self-control. Against such things there is no law (Galatians 5:22-23).

Failure to understand this has caused many people to despair when they don't see sufficient change in their lives. It must be understood that at salvation we change internally, while the outward change will take place as we renew our minds in Christ. I'll elaborate on this later.

Again the word *redeemed* means that you have been rescued from the consequences of sin. This brand-new creation that you are no longer sins. He has rescued you from death. God did not rescue you from sin to leave you in oblivion. He has brought you from death through redemption and has brought you into life by making you a brand-new creation. The life that was robbed from Adam has now been given to you. You are fully, now, and forever a saint.

In this next illustration, there is a significant difference in comparison to the previous diagram. Something has now come into existence that was never there before. We were redeemed.

Who We Are Now in Christ

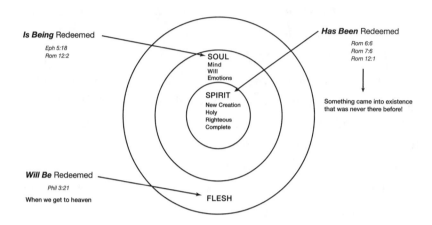

Is Being Redeemed
Eph 5:18
Rom 12:2

Has Been Redeemed
Rom 6:6
Rom 7:6
Rom 12:1

SOUL
Mind
Will
Emotions

SPIRIT
New Creation
Holy
Righteous
Complete

Something came into existence
that was never there before!

Will Be Redeemed
Phil 3:21
When we get to heaven

FLESH

The Spirit

Note that the spirit *has been* redeemed. This means that at one point in the past, the "old man" was crucified with Christ. The "old man" is who we were "in Adam." In short, the "old man" is the web of relationships we maintained in our former life "in Adam." But now, all things have become brand-new. There is no more work for Christ to do in our spirits because *all* things have become new.

Something has occurred—your spirit is now holy, righteous, a new creation, complete, and lacking nothing. You are now a saint and no longer a sinner. You are awesome, and it only makes sense that you should act like a *saint*, one who has the power of God within, because this is who you are.

Paul makes this clear in Romans 1:7: *"To all in Rome who are loved by God and called to be **saints**: Grace and peace to you from God our Father and from the Lord Jesus Christ."*

We Must Know

What must we remember in order to live lives filled with God? Let's search Romans 6 for truth. *"In the same way, count* [consider] *yourselves dead to sin but alive to God in Christ Jesus"* (Rom. 6:11). There are three key words in Romans 6:

1. Know (verses 3,6,9)

2. Consider or Count (verse 11)

3. Present or Yield (verse 13)

It is interesting that the first real command is not found until verse 11. Paul uses the word *consider.* The emphasis in these verses is not upon doing, but upon *knowing* (see Rom. 6:3,6,9,16; 7:1). To have victory, we need to know certain things! It's not that I need to *do* something, but that I need to *know* something.

First, believers must know the truth! This truth is centered upon what Christ has already accomplished by His death and resurrection. The emphasis is *not* upon what I do, but upon what Christ has already done!

Second, believers must have an account of the facts and consider them to be true. Faith is the key! Faith is agreeing with things that we cannot see in the physical and receiving them as true. Faith fixes itself upon the facts of God's Word and counts them as true! Faith says, "Yes it is true. I am dead to sin, and I am living with God! I rejoice in this fact!"

Third, believers in Christ are to present or yield their entire beings to God as those who are alive from the dead (see Rom. 6:13). As new creatures in Christ, it makes complete sense that we will act like who we really are. We are free from sin and death. We are free to give ourselves freely to God. This is why it is imperative that we renew our minds.

The Old Man

Paul speaks about our "old man."

Knowing this, that our old man was crucified with Him, that the body of sin might be done away with, that we should no longer be slaves of sin (Romans 6:6 NKJV).

What is our "old man" (see Rom. 6:6; Eph. 4:22; Col. 3:9), and what is the "new man" (see Col. 3:10; Eph. 4:24)? The "old man" refers to all that I am and all that I have because of Adam; the "new man" refers to all that I am and all that I have because of Christ. The "old man" is my old life in Adam; the "new man" is my new life in Christ. The first refers to the self-life, while the latter refers to the Christ-life. The first has to do with the fallen self; the latter has to do with the redeemed or regenerated self. The "old man" is the old self; the "new man" is the new self, the new creature in Christ.

The "old man" is born of the flesh; the "new man" is born of God. The "old man" came about by natural birth; the "new man" came about by the supernatural new birth. The "new man" is a new thing that did not previously exist, but was created (see Eph. 4:24; 2 Cor. 5:17).

The "old man" will never reform. How then does God deal with the "old man"? God does not change the "old man." God does not transform the "old man." What did God do with your old self? What did God do with all that you are and all that you have in Adam? Romans 6:6 clearly states: *"Our old man **was** crucified with Him."* God condemned the "old man," judged him, and poured out His wrath on him when Jesus died on the cross.

Paul tells us that our "old man" *"was crucified,"* which means it is already done! It is finished! You do not need to re-crucify the "old man"! It is not something that you do; it is something that God has already done! It is not a command to obey; it is a fact to believe!

As a Matter of Fact

Consider this verse:

> *Do not lie to each other, since you have taken off your old self with its practices and have put on the new self, which is being renewed in knowledge in the image of its Creator* (Colossians 3:9-10).

Note carefully the language. It says, *"you have put off"* and *"you have put on."* These are not commands; these are facts. Why has the "old man" been put off? The "old man" has been put off because God put him on the cross! The "new man" has been put on the moment we were saved because we are new creatures in Christ!

Christ's history has become our history because we are in Christ. Thus, His death is our death, His burial is our burial, His resurrection is our resurrection, and His ascension is our ascension.

The Soul

Now make note that our soul realm *is being* redeemed; thus our souls are in process. This simply means that the soul realm is where the work of transformation is taking place. In Ephesians 5:18, Paul teaches us to **keep being filled** with the Holy Spirit. Do you know why we must keep being filled with the Holy Spirit? Because we leak! We forget who we are and who He is. The truth and reality of who we are leaks out of our soul realm. This is why, on a continuum, we must keep being filled with God's presence. Remember, your "soul realm" is in the process of redemption.

Being filled with the Holy Spirit is about agreement with what God has done. When lies permeate our minds, they detract us from the truth and reality that we are God's possessions. Remember, we must believe and agree with Jesus' death, burial, and resurrection. Agreement causes transformation. This is why Romans 12:2 is so important.

> *And do not be conformed to this world, but **be transformed** by the renewing of your mind, so that you may prove what the will of God is, that which is good and acceptable and perfect* (NASB).

The word *transformed* is translated from the word *metamorphosis*. This is what happens to caterpillars as they turn into butterflies.

It is a built-in phenomenon. In every moment, allow yourself to keep being transformed. When we are continually filled with the Holy Spirit, it allows us to keep remembering who He is and who we are (see Eph. 5:18). Our call is to cooperate with the Holy Spirit because transformation is not something that we do, but rather something that happens to us by the Holy Spirit. We will discuss more about the soul in the next chapter.

The Flesh

The flesh *will be* redeemed.

*...who, by the power that enables him to bring everything under his control, will transform our lowly bodies so that they **will be** like his glorious body* (Philippians 3:21).

Until then, let's remember that our flesh carries no spiritual life and is spiritually dead. Since our flesh does not have the mind of Christ, it only has one job description: It is constantly crying out for life! Your flesh is relentlessly crying out for life because it is spiritually dead. Your flesh does not know where to get real life. Your flesh thinks it can get life from physical gratification (pornography), material possessions (houses and cars), fame (church leadership and people's opinions about you), and the list goes on and on. We should not ignore the flesh because it is spiritually dead. On the contrary, we bring it into submission under the brand-new spirit that resides in us.

In the next chapter, we will take a more detailed look at the soul and the flesh.

Summary Questions

1. Read Ezekiel 37:14 in the NIV. What has God promised?

_____

_____

_____

_____

_____

_____

2. Look up the dictionary definition of *redeemed* and write it here.

_____

_____

_____

_____

_____

_____

3. Second Corinthians 5:17 says, "Therefore, if anyone is in Christ, the _____ creation has come; the _____ has gone, the _____ is here."

4. Describe what it means to you to realize that the born-again new you never sins (see page 81).

_____

_____

_____

_____

_____

_____

5. Read First John 1:1-10 in the NIV. Who is John addressing in this passage?

_____

_____

_____

_____

_____

6. What is the point John is driving home in First John 1:1-10? (See page 81-82.)

_____

_____

_____

_____

_____

_____

7. After salvation, what is continually being released into your soul? (See page 83.)

_____

_____

_____

_____

_____

_____

8. Read Galatians 5:22-23 in the NIV. List the fruits of the Spirit:
   a)_____; b)_____; c)_____; d)_____;
   e)_____; f)_____; g)_____; h)_____;
   i)_____.

9. What does the Scripture say about the Law in relation to the fruits of the Spirit?

_____

_____

_____

_____

_____

10. Review the diagram on page 84 and fill in the blanks below.

   The _____ has been redeemed.

   The _____ is being redeemed.

The _____ will be redeemed.

11. Read Romans 6. In light of Romans 6, what must we do to live a life filled with God? (See pages 84-85.)

_____

_____

_____

_____

_____

_____

12. What three key words from Romans 6 are pointed out? (See pages 84-85.)

_____

_____

_____

13. What are three of the things believers need to know in order to have victory? (See page 85.)

_____

_____

_____

_____

_____

_____

_____

_____

14. What does the word *metamorphosis* mean? What part of you is in the process of metamorphosis?

_____

_____

_____

_____

_____

_____

15. If God is responsible for our transformation, what part do we play in the process of transformation?

_____

_____

_____

_____

_____

_____

Endnote

1. *Merriam-Webster's Dictionary,* s.v. "Redeemed"; http://www.merriamwebster.com/dictionary/redeemed (accessed February 17, 2012).

Chapter 7

The Flesh and the
Soul

Your old self is dead and gone.

Let's look at the biblical word *flesh*. The Greek word *sarx* has been translated as "flesh" numerous times in the New Testament.[1] Translated correctly, *sarx* means "flesh, fleshy, or of the flesh." It is important to remember that the flesh is weak, but not automatically sinful. Jesus came to earth in the flesh.

*And the Word **became flesh**, and dwelt among us, and we saw His glory, glory as of the only begotten from the Father, full of grace and truth* (John 1:14 NASB).

But Jesus never did anything according to the flesh. He was simply in bodily physical form. This simply means that Jesus did not do anything in His own self-effort nor did He obtain His sense of worth and value from what He did. In His Spirit, Jesus was completely dependent upon His Father's love and acceptance.

Sarx has three different usages in the New Testament, and it *always* refers to something *natural*, **never** supernatural!

1. It could mean our own self-effort.

Paul confronted the church at Galatia because they were moving in the flesh. They were perfecting (or attempting to complete) their faith through their own self-effort *(sarx/flesh)*. The Galatians wanted to fulfill the requirements of the Law (performance) *and* pursue a relationship with Jesus.

> *You foolish Galatians, who has bewitched you, before whose eyes Jesus Christ was publicly portrayed as crucified? This is the only thing I want to find out from you: did you receive the Spirit by the works of the Law, or by hearing with faith? Are you so foolish? Having begun by the Spirit, **are you now being perfected by the flesh** [self-effort]? Did you suffer so many things in vain-if indeed it was in vain? So then, does He who provides you with the Spirit and works miracles among you, do it by the works of the Law, or by hearing with faith?* (Galatians 3:1-5 NASB).

2. Sarx can also mean "drawing on a natural source for a sense of worth, value, and acceptance."

The Corinthians had a supernatural source in Jesus, but they were drawing on natural sources by identifying themselves with a specific teacher (I am of Paul, I am of Apollos, I am of Cephas). They were using natural sources (people) to draw a sense of value, acceptance, or life. *"And I, brethren, could not speak to you as to spiritual men, but as to men of **flesh**, as to infants in Christ"* (1 Cor. 3:1 NASB).

3. Sarx also refers to the physical body.

We know that Jesus came in the flesh *(sarx)*.

> *And the Word **became flesh**, and dwelt among us, and we beheld His glory, the glory as of the only begotten of the Father, full of grace and truth* (John 1:14 NASB).

Further Understanding of Flesh (Sarx)

Unfortunately, we have lost the true meaning of the word *sarx* because some have taught incorrect theology through sermons, books, songs, and even some Bible translations. In some translations, the word *flesh* has been translated as "sinful man" or "sin nature." As much as I appreciate the New International Version Bible, the translators historically have done the word *sarx* an injustice by translating it as "sinful nature" instead of "flesh." For example, in the 1984 version of the NIV, it reads, *"So I say, live by the Spirit, and you will not gratify the desires of the **sinful nature***" (Gal. 5:16). Fortunately, in the 2010 NIV, *sarx* has been retranslated as "flesh."

However, because of this prevalent mistranslation of *sarx*, many are taught to feel that they have a sin nature. This ill teaching suggests that we have an evil nature that is against God's Spirit, as if we are at odds with God. By contrast, Paul says, *"Therefore having been justified by faith, we have peace with God through our Lord Jesus Christ"* (Rom. 5:1 NKJV).

The King Is Dead

When monarchs transferred power, those who had witnessed the death of one king and the crowning of another, would cry, "The King is dead! Long live the King!" When we initially hear this statement, it can be confusing. How could a king be dead and alive at the same time? They were talking about two different people! Indeed, the former king had died and was no longer king. He had ceased to exist. But the new king, who could never have emerged as king had the old king not died, now lives. So long as the old king remained alive, the new king could not be "born."

But after the second man's "birth" as the new king, the old king could never again resurrect himself and reclaim the throne! The very existence of the one precludes the existence of the other. These two kings cannot jump in and out of the grave and womb, and neither can we. The "old man" has indeed died (see Rom. 6:6). The Holy Spirit has regenerated the "new man" (see Col. 3:10).

Unfortunately, the pervasive position taken by some Christian leaders is that the "old man" is still "alive and well" within the believer and that sinful performance gives daily testimony to this fact. The "old man" is seen to leap in and out of the tomb many times during the typical day.

> ## IT IS IMPOSSIBLE FOR THE "NEW MAN" TO EXIST UNTIL THE "OLD MAN" HAS DIED, AND THE "OLD MAN" CANNOT RESURRECT HIMSELF.

However, one seldom hears a teacher claim that the "new man" leaps in and out of the tomb. The two can't coexist any more than the two kings can! It was the death of the "old man" that enabled the "new man" to be born! It is impossible for the "new man" to exist until the "old man" has died, and the "old man" cannot resurrect himself. Jesus carried resurrection power when He arose from the dead, and His life has been given to you!

Satan must disguise himself if he is to have any hope of victory. He masquerades in the thought lives of Christians by posing as the "old man" and deceiving Christians into thinking that they have a sinful nature by suggesting that they sin. In fact, this causes naïve Christians to direct their defensive efforts against the wrong foe—a darker side of themselves! Christians fire all their bullets at a shadow, instead of at the enemy! This is the explanation for the frustration Paul depicts in Romans 7:15: *"I do not understand what I do. For what I want to do I do not do, but what I hate I do."* We will discuss this at length later.

We know that our old, unrenewed self was nailed to the cross.

> *For we know that our old self was crucified with him so that the body of sin might be done away with,* [made powerless] *that we should no longer be slaves to sin* (Romans 6:6).

So, now that you know that you do not have "two natures," you can no longer say, "I am only human." God has done a supernatural act by giving you a brand-new nature that is now the source of your life.

His Righteousness Given to Us

If we are in Christ, then we have His righteousness, and it is not given to us in degrees. No one receives more or less of it. It is the perfect righteousness of Jesus Christ, and by faith we receive it in its fullness!

We are to measure ourselves by His righteousness alone and not by anyone else's righteousness. Listen to this passage.

We do not dare to classify or compare ourselves with some who commend themselves. When they measure themselves by themselves and compare themselves with themselves, they are not wise. We, however, will not boast beyond proper limits, but will confine our boasting to the field God has assigned to us, a field that reaches even to you (2 Corinthians 10:12-13).

Paul is saying that there is a rule you can use to measure yourself. Everyone who truly repents, believes in the perfect righteousness of Christ, comes to Him in faith, and believes in His work on the cross is made perfectly righteous in the sight of God. We may not have everything worked out yet. Through the power of the Holy Spirit, there is still a daily work of sanctification in our soul realm (see Rom. 12:2). But the Beloved accepts us, and the very righteousness of Christ has been imputed to us!

The Soul Realm and Our Minds

God is transforming our minds. Thus, it is vital to renew the mind.

*Do not conform any longer to the pattern of this world, but be transformed by the **renewing of your mind**. Then you* *will be able to test and approve what God's will is—his good, pleasing and perfect will* (Romans 12:2).

How can we renew our minds? Paul gave us the answer, *"Let this mind be in you, which was also in Christ Jesus"* (Phil. 2:5 NKJV). When we accept Jesus as our Lord and Savior and ask Him to renew our minds, He will gladly do it. In First Corinthians 2:16 we read, *"For who has known the mind of the Lord that he may instruct Him? But we have the mind of Christ."* This literally means we possess Christ's mode of thinking and judging, and we are furnished with His understanding. We are told in this passage that we "have" the mind of Christ, which means that we possess His mind.

This truth becomes who we are; it becomes our worth and character. Power is released when we grasp this truth and allow it to permeate our very souls (our minds, wills, and emotions) and become one with Christ. We have the potential to think His thoughts, His feelings, His purposes, and His desires. This isn't about positive thinking. This is about transformation. This is about allowing God's Word to penetrate into our very spirits, souls, and bodies so that it changes the very substance of who we are. Paul mentions this in his second letter to the Corinthians:

> *Therefore, if anyone is in Christ, he is a new creation; the old has gone, the new is here* (2 Corinthians 5:17).

What is the new that Paul speaks of? The new that has come is present in such things as the mind of Christ, the fruit of the Spirit, anointing, favor, and power. We will have our minds renewed (new pathways carved by the Holy Spirit), and we will continue to experience the effects of being in Christ. Remember, our soul realm is in the process of being sanctified as it catches up with the part of us that is already made perfect, the newly created spirit within us.

 ## LET US LIVE AS PEOPLE WHO HAVE THE MIND OF CHRIST.

Many Christians find themselves living ordinary lives, experiencing neither the presence nor the power of Christ. It is time to receive fresh revelation of who we are in Christ. We need to remember whose mind we truly possess in order to show forth His praises and to powerfully live the abundant life in Christ. We have the extraordinary privilege of boasting in Jesus Christ. Let us live as people who have the mind of Christ. In doing so, we honor His great sacrifice, His great victory, and His great love.

Today, if Jesus is Lord of your life, you have been given a very special gift—His mind! His understanding! His thoughts! His feelings! His purposes! His desires! Celebrate this truth and bask in living an extraordinary life!

The Soul Realm and Our Wills

Our wills are also in the process of metamorphosis (transformation). Our wills are where we make decisions to obey God. We are called to obey, to agree with God, and to act upon the truth. As sons and daughters of God, it only makes sense that we will obey God. When we do not obey God, it is because we are forgetting that we are God's children. Obedience is the manifestation or evidence of knowing God personally. Thus, to change our wills and to bring them into alignment with our new spirits, we must know God.

Meditating on His Word or on His thoughts is possibly the best avenue to gain knowledge of God. I will share more about meditating on God's thoughts later. Paul explains how our wills can agree with the truth or with lies in his letter to the Romans.

> Don't you know that when you offer yourselves to someone to **obey** him as slaves, you are slaves to the one whom you **obey**—whether you are slaves to sin, which leads to death, or to obedience, which leads to righteousness? But thanks be to God that, though you used to be slaves to sin, you wholeheartedly **obeyed** the form of teaching to which you were entrusted. You

have been set free from sin and have become slaves to righteous-ness (Romans 6:16-18).

The Holy Spirit ignites repentance or confession, and He moves us to respond with our wills. Repentance is so pure because it is the goodness of God that draws us to repentance (see Rom. 2:4). There is a significant difference between asking God for forgiveness and repenting. Since we already have complete for-giveness, we need not continue asking God for forgiveness (see Rom. 6:10). Believers should, although, agree with God with a spirit of repentance. Repentance is turning to God (which turns us away from sin) and thanking the One who loves us and has already forgiven us! By doing this, we are agreeing with God that we forgot who we are and that we sinned and mistakenly thought we could get life out of dead things.

The Soul Realm and Our Emotions

Men in particular, especially in our Western culture, have been told that it is wrong to have emotions. This is magnified with statements like, "Real men don't cry!" This communicates that a man is weak if he cries or if he expresses a deep emotion. I would suggest that both Adam and Eve had equal amounts of emotion in the Garden of Eden. I also believe that men and women have equal levels of emotion today, although they may express emotion differently depending on the issue.

Let me explain this. I believe that men have the same amount of emotion as women. Men, however, have been trained to hide their emotions, but emotions have a way of finding their way out. A boiling pot will eventually explode if it has a lid on it.

How do emotions find their way out or explode? Domestic abuse is a definite outgrowth of stifled emotions. While women can also become abusers, men are often the ones who abuse. Abusers use fear, guilt, shame, and intimidation to wear people down and keep them under their thumb. Abusers also use physical abuse such as rape, physical pain, punching holes in walls, and so on. Let me share a story with you about stifled emotions.

I met a friend of mine, Michael, in a coffee shop one day. He shared with me that he had grown up being trained to stifle his emotions.

I asked Michael, "How were you trained to stifle your emotions?"

Michael said, "It was easy. My dad would immediately lift his hand up with a threat to hit me any time that I cried as a little boy. He would holler out, 'Stop that crying, or I will give you something to cry about.' This triggered an ability to stifle my emotions; thus, I began to shut down emotionally."

Every time Michael was told to stop crying, it made him suppress his emotions. Over time, he learned to shut his emotions down and to stop feeling altogether.

While other men might not have experienced the same scenario that Michael did, the messages that men receive in our culture have trained them to stifle their real emotions. Anyone who has heard these messages has slowly trained himself or herself to stop feeling emotions. But again, emotions never get stifled; they just find other ways to rise up.

Shame Is an Emotion

We stand in front of our mirrors each and every day and make statements: "I'm too fat," "My nose is too big," "My hair is fading away," "My face is covered with acne," or "No one could really love me." These are statements of indictment. They are emotions based on lies. We often define how we feel about ourselves through lies. This is called shame-based thinking. This thinking is based on the fact that we believe we are defective, unlovable, and inadequate. While this is not true, if we believe it is, it will affect our ability to receive from God as His Bride.

The Skills of Shame

In order to survive in a shame-based life, people have to learn certain skills, such as perfection, lying, or performance, which enable them to exist and avoid hopelessness.

When shame controls your emotions, you definitely do not want to make mistakes in front of people. People who struggle with shame always need to supply a reason for their mistakes. They avoid taking ownership for their own faults and shift blame to others. When their children misbehave in front of family or friends, they fear being judged as a bad parent. Failing to maintain certain religious ideals makes them feel like a defective Christian. People who struggle with shame cannot observe their friends and family receiving a new car, house, or furniture without concluding that God must love them more. People who walk in shame are afraid to express different opinions for fear of appearing stupid or inadequate.

Church Leaders Mean Well?

Many years ago, my wife, kids, and I attended a small church in Redding, California. We were new Christians at the time.

The pastor would offer an altar call every week, and my wife would go forward in tears just about every week. On the outside, I was appearing to be very supportive of her tearful approaches to God, but on the inside I was screaming, "These people must think I am the worst husband in the world!"

One week the leaders in the church called me up front and gathered around me. Now remember, at this point I was a brand-new Christian. As the leaders gathered, they said, "You know, Ken, that your wife comes forward each week in tears."

I responded, "Yes, I have been praying for her when she goes forward."

They continued, "Ken, as the spiritual leader in your home, we want you to be aware that you carry the responsibility for your wife's spiritual well-being."

I agreed with them. As a brand-new believer, this made sense to me because my spiritual leaders had taught me that this was the way Jesus intended it to be.

They counseled, "You need to be in the Word of God more, you need to give more, and you need to be a better husband and father."

I agreed, and the very next morning I was off to the races. I got up at 6:00 a.m. to read the Bible. I did this for the next two weeks. At the time, I did not understand that weekly requests for prayer and tears at the altar were a sign that God was working deeply in Becky's life. I misunderstood the situation and thought that there was no change since she continued to cry freely. So I decided to get up an additional hour earlier every day to read the Scriptures. A couple of weeks later, there were still no changes. So I continued to try to fix Becky through performance by giving more money to the church, and you guessed it, there was still no change.

There Was a Problem

While I was being manipulated by spiritual leaders (who I am sure meant well and who only treated me this way because this was all they knew), that was not the original problem. The original problem was that my emotions began to agree with those lies. I believed the lie that said I was a lousy husband because my wife was a mess, not to mention the lie that said my church family would not accept me even if I was a lousy husband. I was definitely trying to get spiritual life out of things that could not produce life. I was attempting to produce change through works rather than trusting God and inviting His liberating and healing presence into the situation.

The next problem was that my spiritual leaders were leading me into performance-based Christianity that did not help my wife's transformation. I was more concerned with keeping people happy with me than I was about my wife. I found myself being catapulted into maximum performance.

Because I was a young believer who didn't understand how to submit my emotions to the Holy Spirit, the unhealthy spiritual counsel I was receiving was amplified in my life, and I walked deeply into performance-based Christianity. I know now that my wife's spiritual condition was not my fault; but instead of directing my spiritual energy into prayer and encouragement to her, I spiraled into performance. Because I did not understand that I am forgiven, loved, and accepted as Christ's Bride, my energy was focused on trying to earn these things from Him. I was in need of a total identity makeover from God!

God Aligns Our Emotions

Our emotions are being changed by the power of God. The word *emotion* has several definitions. According to the *Merriam-Webster's Dictionary*, the Latin root of the word *emotion* means, "to displace."[2] I find that definition very interesting because that is what carnal, uncrucified emotions try to do. They displace us and move us away from God. This is exactly what Adam and Eve did the moment they forgot who they were: they hid. In fact, Satan's plan is to get us to live by our carnal feelings so we never walk in the Spirit. God created us to experience His emotions and our emotions. He is an emotional God. This does not make Him weak; it simply means that He has healthy and truth-based feelings about us.

Remember that feelings are neither right nor wrong, and they are perfectly okay to have. While it is okay to experience feelings, they do not always line up with the truth of God. Many of us have been, or know individuals who have been, controlled by their emotions. These people make most of their decisions based on how they feel at any given moment. Unfortunately, since our emotions do not always line up with the truth of God, we are often under their control, which can lead us into more lies. We can, however, submit our emotions to the control of the Holy Spirit so that they will agree with the truth of God.

How Far Is the East from the West?

So how much are you forgiven? Let me use an analogy to explain. If you traveled north in an airplane with the intent of traveling around the earth, what direction would you be traveling after you crossed over the North Pole? You would be traveling south, even if initially you started traveling north. If you travel south around the earth, you will eventually start traveling north when you move beyond the South Pole.

What is amazing is that when you travel eastward, you will always be traveling east; you will never be traveling west. Conversely, if you take off in the same plane and travel west, you will continue traveling west.

Aren't you glad that your sins *are not* forgiven as far as the north is from the south! But your sins are eternally forgiven as far as the *east* is from the *west*. Hallelujah!

God's Promises Are True

Listen to the prophet Ezekiel express the Father's heart.

Then I will sprinkle clean water on you, and you will be clean; I will cleanse you from all your filthiness and from all your idols. Moreover, I will give you a new heart and put a new Spirit within you; and I will remove the heart of stone from your flesh and give you a heart of flesh. I will put My Spirit within you

*and cause you to walk in My statutes, and you will be careful to
observe My ordinances* (Ezekiel 36:25-27 NASB).

Did you notice the additional promise that God makes toward
us? He promises to give us a brand-new heart and to place a
brand-new spirit in us. He will make us clean and *we will* obey
Him. While we are responsible to cooperate with God's leadership, God Himself will be in charge of our new and consistent
behavior. Always remember that God is not going to force Himself upon anyone. He is looking for voluntary lovers who will
invite Him to change their behaviors to align and be consistent
with who we are to Him.

My favorite verse concerning the revelation of our identity as
the Bride is *"Let us **keep living** by the same standard to which **we
have attained"*** (Phil. 3:16 NASB). I note a couple of things in
this verse. First, we are to keep *living*. It doesn't say that we are
to keep *dying* (to the flesh or to the sinful nature within us). Second, we have already attained the standard of Jesus because we
have died to our old selves (once and for all) and we now live for
Christ! We are to soar consistently on the outside because of who
we already are on the inside.

The Greek word for "sin" is *harmatia*, which means "missing the mark."[3] While this is biblically sound, I have a practical
definition that I have adopted and can truly relate to. I define
sin as "trying to get spiritual life out of things or actions that are
incapable of producing life because of being unaware or having
forgotten one's identity as a child of the life-giving God." In short,
sin is the result of forgetting who we are or trying to get life out
of dead things!

One of my original mentors, Jeff VanVonderon, wrote a powerful book entitled *Tired of Trying to Measure Up*. In his book, Jeff
has a brilliant statement defining sin. "Anyone or anything from
which you and I try to acquire life, value and meaning, outside of
the true God, is a false god."[4]

Why Not Put the "Flesh to Death"?

If you have to put the flesh to death (die to self), then it's you doing it, and that is self-effort. Why would you have to put the flesh to death when the flesh is already dead? The goal of the Christian life is not to stop sinning. The goal of the believer's life is to keep remembering who you are, that you are permanently stationed at the banqueting table. The "old self" (see Rom. 6:6) can no more be re-crucified than Christ can be, and even if it could be, you couldn't do it!

The fact that Jesus came in the flesh does not make Him automatically sinful. It does not mean that He had a sinful nature. Jesus always looked to His Father as His source for life, strength, purpose, and desire. Even when Satan came and tempted Jesus to look to natural things to meet His needs, He never turned to those natural things to meet His needs. He *lived in the flesh*, but never did things *according to the flesh*. He walked according to His Father, who was always His source for everything.

Before we were Christians, we were in the flesh, and we also did things according to the flesh (the flesh was our source for life). We tried quite unsuccessfully to get life out of dead things such as money, status, inappropriate sex, and people's opinions. And even though the flesh never delivered, we kept trying because we did things according to the flesh.

People actually become Christians when they begin to get their life from God. His Spirit is the only source that can give us life. When we get life from the Spirit at the time of salvation, the natural flesh is no longer our source. Galatians 5:24 clearly states this fact, *"Now those who belong to Christ Jesus **have crucified** the flesh with its passions and desires"* (NASB). Paul clearly emphasizes this truth again in his letter to the Galatians.

> I **have been** crucified with Christ and I no longer live, but
> Christ lives in me. The life I live in the flesh, I live by faith in the

Son of God, who loved me and gave himself for me (Galatians 2:20).

The Last Samurai

In the magnificent movie *The Last Samurai*, Tom Cruise plays a character by the name of Algren, an ex-United States Army Captain. In the movie, the westernized Japanese Imperial Army recruits Algren, because he is a decorated warrior, to help train their soldiers to defeat the ancient samurai warriors.

Within days of his arrival in Japan, Algren is informed that he must quickly train the Japanese army for immediate battle with the samurai. Algren obstinately tells the head of the Japanese army that the troops are not ready for any battle, much less against the ancient samurai warriors who rely solely on their swords and armor. He had been training the Japanese soldiers on the use of American guns and ammunition and recognized they were not proficient yet. It was obvious that the samurai were superior warriors and that the Imperial army would be easily defeated.

Algren is reluctantly forced into battle with his unprepared army. They battle against each other until the samurai warriors defeat the Imperial army and take Algren captive.

During the battle, Chief Samurai Katsumoto notices Algren's valiant skills and great passion to survive. As a result, the chief samurai befriends Algren while he is confined at the samurai camp. Over the next year, Algren is captivated with the samurai lifestyle and becomes very skilled in samurai warfare.

During the brutal, final battle scene of the movie, most of the samurai die, including Katsumoto, who becomes known as the last samurai. Algren is also wounded and in deep emotional pain because his good friend, Katsumoto, has died at the hands of the Japanese army.

A few days later, Algren presents Katsumoto's sword to the young Japanese emperor. As Algren walks up to the young Emperor, he respectfully bows and lowers his head. As Algren is frozen in his submitted pose, he offers up the last samurai's sword to the young emperor.

The young emperor says, "Tell me, how did he die?"

Algren looks into his eyes and—with great pain and agony—says, "I will not tell you how he died. I will tell you how he lived."

It Is Time for the Truth

My friends, it is time for the Bride of Christ to stop telling everyone how he or she has died to the flesh or the sinful nature. We need to start telling everyone how we live for God. We are alive because Jesus rose from the dead. So let us start remembering that the flesh is dead and start focusing our lives in Christ.

Romans 6:11-14 says:

> *In the same way,* **count yourselves dead to sin but alive to God in Christ Jesus.** *Therefore do not let sin reign in your mortal body so that you obey its evil desires. Do not offer the parts of your body to sin, as instruments of wickedness,* **but rather offer yourselves to God, as those who have been brought from death to life; and offer the parts of your body to him as instruments of righteousness.** *For sin shall not be your master, because you are not under law, but under grace.*

Yes and Amen!

Summary Questions

1. What is the correct translation of the Greek word *sarx?* (See page 93)

_____

_____

_____

_____

_____

_____

2. Is the following statement true or false? "Flesh is automatically sinful." True / False (See page 93.)

3. *Sarx* always refers to something _____, never
   _____. (See page 93.)

4. List the three different usages of *sarx* in the New Testament
   (see pages 93-94).

_____

_____

_____

_____

_____

_____

_____

_____

_____

5. Romans 6:6-7: "For we know that our _____ self was crucified with him so that the body ruled by sin might be done
   away with, that we should no longer be slaves to _____—
   because anyone who has ___ has been set _____ _____
   _____ " (NIV).

6. Write out what you believe Romans 6:6-7 means (see pages
   95-97).

_____

_____

_____

_____

7. What had to "die" for the "new man" to have life? (See pages 95-97.)

8. Do you have two natures or one new nature? Why? (See page 97.)

Endnotes

1. Thayer and Smith, *The KJV New Testament Greek Lexicon*, s.v. "Sarx" (#4561); BibleStudyTools.com; http://www.biblestudytools.com/lexicons/greek/kjv/sarx.html (accessed February 17, 2012).

2. *Merriam-Webster's Dictionary*, s.v. "Emotion"; http://http://www.merriam-webster.com/dictionary/emotion (accessed February 17, 2012).

3. Thayer and Smith, *The KJV New Testament Greek Lexicon*, s.v. "Hamartia" (#266); BibleStudyTools.com; http://

www.biblestudytools.com/lexicons/greek/kjv/hamartia. html (accessed February 17, 2012).

4. Jeff VanVonderon, *Tired of Trying to Measure Up* (Minneapolis, MN: Bethany House Publishers, 1990), 101.

Chapter 8

What Shall We Say, Then?

*We have been brought from an old country into a
brand-new country*

The kingdom of God is about agreement. We either agree
with the truth of God or the lies of the enemy. There really
is no in between.

Paul tells us something very important in his letter to the
Roman church. When he penned this letter, he didn't break it
into verses—it was one continuous thought. Verses have been
added to make biblical addresses more coherent. Therefore, we
can read Romans 5:18–6:18 as one thought. Let's take a look at
part of that passage.

> *For just as through the disobedience of the one man the many
> were made sinners, so also through the obedience of the one man
> the many will be made righteous. The law was added so that the
> trespass might increase. But where sin increased, grace increased
> all the more, so that, just as sin reigned in death, so also grace
> might reign through righteousness to bring eternal life through
> Jesus Christ our Lord. What shall we say, then? Shall we go on*

*sinning so that grace may increase? By no means! We died to sin;
how can we live in it any longer?* (Romans 5:19–6:2)

Paul says *"God has brought eternal life through the righteousness of
Jesus."* Because of what Jesus has done (see Rom. 5:19), should
we continue to sin so that grace might abound (see Rom. 6:1)?
No way. How can we who have been saved from sin still live like
sinners? We have been brought from an old country into a brand-
new country. How can we go back to the old country? We are
now and forevermore saints. We are no longer sinners!

HOW CAN WE GO BACK TO THE OLD COUNTRY?

I heard Kris Vallotton from Bethel Church in Redding, California, once say, "If we believe we are sinners, then we will sin by
faith!" We function and move based upon what we believe. We
have to remember who we are. Proverbs 23:7a lets us know that
"as he [a person] *thinks within himself, so he is"* (NASB). If we choose
to agree with the lie that says we are nothing but sinners saved
by grace, then we will continue to live in sin. We will not experience the freedom from sin that being a slave to righteousness has
brought us. Try arguing with the truth of First John 3:9:

No one who is born of God will continue to sin, ***because
God's seed remains in him; he cannot go on sinning****, because he has been born of God.*

It is no longer our nature to sin because our old selves are dead
and gone. We do not have a sin nature. We need to remember that
our old selves are dead. Our very nature has been changed. The
truth of the matter is that we are good because God is good, and
He has given us new spirits and new minds (see Ezek. 36:26; 1 Cor.
2:16). We actually think like Jesus because we have His mind!

WE NO LONGER NEED TO KEEP DYING TO FLESH, BUT TO KEEP LIVING IN CHRIST.

We have been baptized into the same death that Christ endured. And we have been raised from the dead just like Christ. Our old selves were co-crucified with Christ so that sin would become powerless. Sin has no more clout with us. We live with Christ.

We no longer need to keep dying to flesh, but we do need to keep living in Christ. Death is no longer master over Jesus because He died once and for all; therefore, we count ourselves dead to sin and alive to Christ. We no longer allow the travesty of sin to reign in our bodies. Sin is no longer master over us. We are holy, righteous, and new creations full of the Spirit of God. We are not under the Law any more, for we are now under His powerful grace. We do not choose to sin because we are under His grace. On the contrary, we choose righteousness because we have God's grace that empowers us to live lives full of power.

Let's break down these verses in the book of Romans to see the truth they communicate:

> *Or don't you know that all of us who were baptized into Christ Jesus were baptized into his death? We were therefore buried with him through baptism into death in order that, just as Christ was raised from the dead through the glory of the Father, we too may live a new life* (Romans 6:3-4).

In these verses, Paul reflects on the fact that Christians have a different understanding of the Law because of their faith in Christ. The Law binds the living, not the dead. This concept is exemplified in marriage, which binds two people together in life, but is dissolved through death. Similarly, Christians who have died with Christ to sin through baptism are freed from the Law that produced sin, which in turn brought about death. Now that Christians are joined to Christ, the power of Christ's resurrection makes it possible for them to bear the fruit of newness of life in God.

> *If we have been united with him like this in his death, we will certainly also be united with him in his resurrection. For we know that our old self was crucified with him so that the body of sin might be done away with, that we should no longer be slaves to sin—because anyone who has died has been set free from sin* (Romans 6:5-7).

The word *united* means we have become just like Him in His death, burial, and resurrection. I do not often use the King James translation, but it is helpful to look at these verses in that version. It is a must read!

> *For if we have been **planted together** in the likeness of his death, we shall be also in the likeness of his resurrection* (Romans 6:5-7 KJV).

This *"planted together"* would represent one plant being rooted in another plant so that the first plant derives its strength and life from the second plant. A good example of this reality is the Spanish Moss that grows on trees in the southern part of the United States. The moss is a distinct species, but it only grows as part of another tree; it cannot exist alone. It derives its life from the life of another.

We are planted in Christ's death and resurrection. Since we have death through Jesus, our life is also found in Him alone. I have a life, but I would cease to exist spiritually if I was cut off from His life. Jesus reminds us of this great truth and promise in John's gospel:

> *If you remain in me and my words remain in you, ask whatever you wish, and it will be given you. This is to my Father's glory, that you bear much fruit, showing yourselves to be my disciples* (John 15:7-8).

Let's go back to the book of Romans:

For we know that our old self was crucified with him so that the body of sin might be done away with... (Romans 6:6).

The words *"done away with"* remind us that our old selves have died and have been made permanently impotent. They are utterly powerless. Spiritual fruit can only be produced with and through resurrection power, not self-power. I cannot decide to bear fruit; I must bear it through Him, because we are walking in resurrection life. This is the same power and the same life that Christ had when He was raised from the dead. Being born again is no less miraculous!

Since you have been raised with Christ, set your heart on things above, where Christ is seated at the right hand of God. In other words, set your mind on things above, not on earthly things. Since your old self has died, your life is now hidden in Christ (see Col. 3:1-4). Since you walk in resurrection power, you can also set your mind on resurrection things. Since you have also partaken in Christ's ascension, your home is now nothing less than heaven itself.

Let's continue:

Now if we died with Christ, we believe that we will also live with him. For we know that since Christ was raised from the dead, he cannot die again; death no longer has mastery over him. The death he died, he died to sin once for all; but the life he lives, he lives to God (Romans 6:8-10).

These verses tell us that we have been freed from sin. The power of sin is broken in my life and in yours. But again, you may ask, "Why do I still sin?" The reason you choose to sin is simple. You forgot who you are. Remember, your "soul realm" is still in the process of redemption. Your mind, will, and emotions thought you could get life out of dead things. You thought you could get life out of something or someone other than God.

Remember, the brand-new you (the place where God now dwells) no longer sins. Christ made you holy, righteous, and a brand-new creation. Because of what Christ did for you, you are now free to not sin. You now have the amazing privilege to choose life, which is something you did not previously have.

Remember the illustration of "Who We Are Now in Christ."

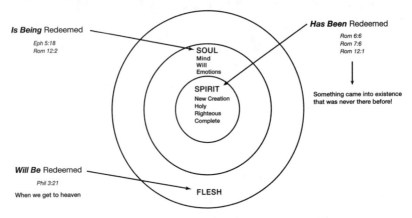

The Spirit of God dwells in the brand-new you, and because you are brand-new, you no longer sin. This is simply because God's light is constantly shining on the new you, and there is no sin where the light of God is shining. But the "soul realm" (mind, will, and emotions) is still in the process of being transformed. This is the realm where we forget who we are and sin. God is in the process of renewing our minds into the reality of the kingdom of God. This is the realm where God is making us more like His Son Jesus.

 ## YOU ARE NOW LIVING FOR GOD AND SIN IS A FOREIGN LAND FOR YOU.

Once again, we can see why Paul drives home to us in Romans 12:2 that we are to renew our minds and to be transformed. This is why we do not have to keep dying, but only to keep remembering who we are.

Since Christ cannot die again, and He died to sin once and for all, you do not have to keep dying. You are now living!

Now let's take a look at the next couple of verses:

In the same way, count yourselves dead to sin but alive to God in Christ Jesus. Therefore do not let sin reign in your mortal body so that you obey its evil desires (Romans 6:11-12).

Christ died once and for all; He will never die again. The same is true for you. Continuing to die does not make sense because you are forever alive to Christ.

I Die Daily

Most of us have been taught the doctrine of dying daily to our flesh. This teaching is often based upon Paul's words to the Corinthians: *"I affirm, by the boasting in you which I have in Christ Jesus our Lord, I die daily"* (1 Cor. 15:31 NKJV). Teachers assert that if Paul died daily then we should as well. Let's take a closer look at the context in which Paul spoke these words. The phrase *"die daily"* means, "every day I am in the danger of death." The Greek word for "die daily" is *apothnesko.*[1] These words are speaking of natural death, not spiritual death or dying to self or the flesh.

Paul was proclaiming that his physical life was on the line each and every day for the sake of the resurrection of Christ and all believers. Listen to Paul's words just a few verses earlier:

But if it is preached that Christ has been raised from the dead, how can some of you say that there is no resurrection of the dead? If there is no resurrection of the dead, then not even Christ has been raised. And if Christ has not been raised, our preaching is useless and so is your faith. More than that, we are then found to be false witnesses about God, for we have testified about God that he raised Christ from the dead... (1 Corinthians 15:12-15).

Paul continues:

Now if there is no resurrection, what will those do who are bap-
tized for the dead? If the dead are not raised at all, why are people
baptized for them? ***And as for us, why do we endanger***
ourselves every hour? I face death every day —
yes, just as surely as I boast about you in Christ Jesus our Lord.
If I fought wild beasts in Ephesus with no more than human
hopes, what have I gained? If the dead are not raised, "Let us
eat and drink, for tomorrow we die (1 Corinthians 15:29-32).

If you want to agree with Paul that your physical life is on the
line for the resurrection, go for it. Some people put their lives on
the line for the gospel frequently, those in countries like China
and in cities like Cairo, Egypt. And there may come a time when
Americans will put their physical lives on the line as well. We cannot, however, use First Corinthians 15:31 to theologically support
why we are to die to self or to the flesh.

We Must Consider

The reason we Christians sin is due to the nature of our unrenewed minds, not because we have a sin nature. We must "count"
or consider ourselves dead to sin. But again you say, "But I still
sin!" You are focusing on the wrong issue. You must not focus on
sin or be self-conscious. You must be God-conscious! If you sin
and forget who you are, repent to God and don't dwell on it.

The fact that you *know* you have sinned means that the power
of sin is broken in your life. You simply forgot who you are. I have
heard people say, "If I don't focus on stopping my sin, I am ignor-
ing the truth that I still sin, and I will continue to sin." When the
concentration is on trying to stop sinning, we have missed the
mark. We are going to have to take God at His Word and refocus
our minds on Him, not on sin. After all, God reminds us: *"So I*
say, walk by the Spirit, and you will not gratify the desires of the flesh"
(Gal. 5:16).

You are now living for God, and sin is a foreign land for you. You may visit there, but you are an alien, a foreigner. You know where you live, and that land is resurrection land.

> *Do not offer the parts of your body to sin, as instruments of wickedness, but rather offer yourselves to God, as those who have been brought from death to life; and offer the parts of your body to him as instruments of righteousness. For sin shall not be your master, because you are not under law, but under grace* (Romans 6:13-14).

Verse 13 is a command. *"Do not offer the parts of your body to sin, as instruments of wickedness...."* Since this is a command, God has also released His power to empower us to stop sinning. God would never give us a command that is not possible to carry out. Yet, without the Spirit's presence in our lives, we would not be able to even consider doing this. God has given each of us the choice to not sin. Since we are His children, we will choose life versus death and sin. Paul continues in verse 14 when he states that there is no law that can conquer sin, but God's grace gives us the power to live victoriously.

> *What then? Shall we sin because we are not under law but under grace? By no means! Don't you know that when you offer yourselves to someone to obey him as slaves, you are slaves to the one whom you obey—whether you are slaves to sin, which leads to death, or to obedience, which leads to righteousness? But thanks be to God that, though you used to be slaves to sin, you wholeheartedly obeyed the form of teaching to which you were entrusted. You have been set free from sin and have become slaves to righteousness* (Romans 6:15-18).

Verse 15 clearly tells us that we do not sin so that grace can come into our lives. That would be like becoming sick so you can take more medication. If you are **not** sick, you do not need medication. Don't you remember that you are living in a brand-new country called *Grace*?

Based upon verse 16, it seems to me that it is your choice as to who you will serve. But then, the one whom you serve will produce power and influence over your life. If you choose sin, it will dominate you, and you will be its slave. If you choose obedience, then the power of the Spirit will dominate you, and you will serve Him. The choice is yours. As a child of God, have you chosen to obey?

It would seem that you are destined to be a "slave." It is just a matter of who will be your master. If you choose not to be a slave of Christ, then you are not free; you are simply a slave to the power of sin. But, since Christ raised you from the dead, you are free indeed, and you can choose to obey Him. It only makes sense that you would! Listen to Paul's comments:

> *But thanks be to God that, though **you used to be** slaves to sin, you have come to obey from your heart the pattern of teaching that has now claimed your allegiance* (Romans 6:17).

Because of who you are, give thanks to the one who has given you a brand-new name. The Hebrew word *Hephzibah*, in Isaiah 62:4, means "my delight is in her."

> *No longer will they call you Deserted, or name your land Desolate. But you will be called **Hephzibah**, and your land Beulah; for the LORD will take delight in you, and your land will be married.*

God is always delighted with you. You are a perfect Bride for His Son. Listen to Paul carefully articulate this truth that they should be focused on God and God alone.

> *I am using an example from everyday life because of your human limitations. Just as you used to offer yourselves as slaves to impurity and to ever-increasing wickedness, so now offer yourselves as slaves to righteousness leading to holiness. When you were slaves to sin, you were free from the control of righteousness. What benefit did you reap at that time from the things you are now ashamed of? Those things result in death! But now that you have been set free from sin and have become slaves to God, the benefit you reap*

leads to holiness, and the result is eternal life. For the wages of sin is death, but the gift of God is eternal life in Christ Jesus our Lord (Romans 6:19-23).

In these verses, Paul is simply communicating that you cannot get life out of dead stuff! Notice that Paul is referring to the past as he writes to the Roman Christians, *"Just as you* **used to...** *When you* **were** *slaves to sin...What benefit* **did you reap at that time** *from the things that you are now ashamed of?"* All of those things brought about death because they are things of the flesh. And the flesh can only deliver death!

Then Paul speaks about the present and the future: *"But now that you have been set free from sin...."* Paul indicates that sin is no longer in control of our lives. We are now slaves to God. God has delivered us into life with Him. We have eternal life. The word *eternal* speaks not only of the future, but it also refers to the now; it is now and forevermore.

When we remember this truth, it will set us free. We are free to move in the power of miracles and signs and wonders. Evidence of this kind of power will provoke us to preach, proclaim, prophesy, and speak of His redeeming love to lost, hurting, and pain-filled people. As we unite with God and agree with Him, we are filled with the Holy Spirit, and we move out under His grace and power. We then begin to notice that God designed us to experience life full of His Spirit and to walk in abundance.

Joint Heirs with Christ

It only makes sense that, as brand-new creations, we should give ourselves to Him. We are His sons and daughters. We are joint heirs with Christ. As joint heirs with Christ, we get everything that Christ has. The beauty of the bridal paradigm message is that we have our inheritance, now! The difference between earthly and heavenly inheritances is that we do not have to wait for God's inheritance.

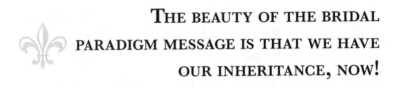

The Beauty of the Bridal Paradigm Message Is That We Have Our Inheritance, Now!

To receive an earthly inheritance, someone has to die. Christ has already died; therefore, we get our inheritance now. Christ has already placed the inheritance in our account. Our inheritance is waiting for us to make a withdrawal. But we will *not* make a withdrawal *until* we understand that we *now* have the privilege to activate such a withdrawal as sons and daughters of God!

God desires that we occupy every spiritual territory. He desires that we be occupied with His power, authority, and love. God desires us to constantly be expanding. This is what Jesus meant when He taught us to pray, *"Your kingdom come, your will be done on earth as it is in heaven"* (Matt. 6:10). A spiritual inheritance makes us more effective and efficient in representing the King and His kingdom. A spiritual inheritance pulls back the curtain and reveals what we already have permission to use and to take possession of the earth. We will discuss this in more detail later.

Do You Agree?

Do you agree that it is possible to go 24 hours without sinning? Jesus did, and He is our perfect illustration of a life full of the presence of God. Remember that as a man Jesus showed us a life entirely dependent on His Father. He depended on His Father for everything and did not do anything that His Father did not lead Him to do. Jesus was in utter dependence on His Father. Jesus did not demand Himself equal to God, but chose to become a man unto death. Jesus was fully secure in His Father's love, acceptance, and purposes. Take a careful look at what Paul said to the Philippians.

...Have the same mindset as Christ Jesus: Who, being in very nature God, did not consider equality with God something to be used to his own advantage; rather, he made himself nothing, by taking the very nature of a servant, being made in human likeness. And being found in appearance as a man, he humbled himself by becoming obedient to death—even death on a cross! Therefore God exalted him to the highest place and gave him the name that is above every name, that at the name of Jesus every knee should bow, in heaven and on earth and under the earth, and every tongue acknowledge that Jesus Christ is Lord, to the glory of God the Father (Philippians 2:5-11).

Notice that we are to have the same mindset (earlier versions of the NIV say "attitude") as Christ, which means that we should depend on our Father just as Christ depended on His Father—not because we ought to, but because it makes sense that we should. This is simply who we are! Believers in Christ lean into the arms of a loving God, looking at Him and to Him for everything they need. Jesus, while He was God, chose to completely lay down His heavenly nature. He actually took on the very nature of a servant, even to the point of dying on a cross. Because Jesus was a man, He leaned into His Father for all things, and because of this, His Father has exalted Him to the highest of places and given Him the name that is above all other names!

A Dog and His Bone

Once a boy tried to take a bone from a dog. Unwilling to let go of his bone, the dog bit him. His father said, "Here, let me take the bone away from the dog." Soon the father came back to where the boy was standing and held out the bone to him. His son asked, "How did you do that, Dad?" His father smiled and said, "I gave him something he wanted more than the bone; I gave him a steak."

It's easy to give up sin when you have something better!

God has either made it possible for us to go for 24 hours without sinning, or this Christianity and all that God has purposed to do through the blood and sacrifice of His Son is a big waste of time. Not only that, but God would have to be a liar.

We are active pursuers of Christ; therefore, we will not grab hold of death, but life. Since God never lies, I am willing to tell you that you can walk deeper and deeper into Him and experience 24 hours without sinning and have an abundant life full of the Spirit.

Now that you know that you are a joint heir with Christ and that you are no longer a sinner, but a saint, let's take a look at why God gave Israel the Mosaic Law and what its purpose was and is.

Summary Questions

1. The kingdom of God is about _____. We either agree with the _____ of God or the _____ of the enemy (see page 113).

2. What activities assist in the renewing of our minds? (See page 117.)

_____

_____

_____

_____

_____

_____

3. "As he [a person] _____ within himself, so he _____" (Prov. 23:7a NASB).

4. What does it mean to have the mind of Christ?

_____

_____

_____

_____

_____

_____

5. How do you know the power of sin is broken in your life? (See page 120-121.)

_____

_____

_____

_____

_____

6. Write what the following statement means to you: You are living in a brand-new country called Grace (see pages 120-121).

_____

_____

_____

_____

_____

7. Do you agree that it's possible to go 24 hours without sinning? Write out your thoughts on this. (See page 126.)

_____

_____

_____

_____

_____

8. Read Philippians 2:5-11. What does this passage mean to you? Whose attitude should yours be like and why? (See pages 124-125.)

_____

_____

_____

_____

_____

_____

Endnote

1. Thayer and Smith, *The NAS New Testament Greek Lexicon,* s.v. "Apothnesko" (#599); BibleStudyTools.com, http://www.biblestudytools.com/lexicons/greek/nas/apoth-nesko.html (accessed February 17, 2012).

Chapter 9

Do You Think the Law Is Good?

Each time the Pharisees would tout that they had
not sinned, Jesus would give them more Law.

On the cross, Jesus received all of the Law's condemnation and judgment. We died with Him to the Law, and it can, therefore, no longer condemn us. We now serve God in an altogether different way, not through laws, but through the heart. Since we are no longer under the Law, does the Law actually accomplish anything?

Indeed, if the Law brings us into bondage, could not it be said that the Law and sin are equally evil? One promotes the other. The Apostle Paul anticipates this question and asks the Romans, "Is the Law sin?" (See Romans 7:7.) Paul graciously answers the question with a profound explanation of the purpose of the Law.

The Law Reveals Sin

The Law makes us conscious of sin (see Rom. 3:20). The Law was also given to reveal the holiness of God. We live in a culture where a clear conscience is very rare and almost anything goes. Unmarried couples live together and sleep together; we adjust our tax returns; we murder unborn children in the womb; and lying, drunkenness, and drugs are all commonplace. These are acceptable practices in American culture and throughout the earth.

EACH TIME THE PHARISEES WOULD TOUT THEY HAD NOT SINNED, JESUS WOULD GIVE THEM MORE LAW.

God's Law presents humanity with a definite statement of right and wrong. The Pharisees thought they were acting holy and avoiding sin because their perception of sin was that it could be measured by outward expressions of deeds. So they tried to argue with Jesus by saying they had not committed adultery. But Jesus reminded them:

> *You have heard that it was said, "Do not commit adultery," but I tell you that anyone who looks at a woman lustfully has already committed adultery with her in his heart* (Matthew 5:27-28).

Jesus kept giving more Law. Each time the Pharisees would tout that they had not sinned, Jesus would give them more Law. The Law was truly given to reveal sin in the heart of humanity and to reveal the holiness of God.

The Law Provokes Sin

There is a beautiful wooded area right next to The Prayer House in Chico, California. Many people go on walks and spend time next to the creek eating lunch and enjoying each other's company. Many people also bring their dogs to let them walk, run, play, and exercise. I have noticed that there is no sign anywhere on the property telling the owners of these dogs to have them on a leash. Suppose that the city of Chico suddenly decided to make the park a "dogs must be on a leash" park. Imagine dog owners arriving at the park and immediately letting their dogs run and exercise as they part from their vehicles. Then shortly, as they walk through the park, they notice a sign staked in the ground that says: "Dogs Must Be On A Leash!" The immediate reaction from the dog owner is to rebel. "My dog is well-behaved; he will stay next to me. I do not need to have him on a leash. And by the way, this sign was not here the other day." A little farther down the path, there is another signed staked in the ground stating; you guessed it, "Dogs Must Be On A Leash." There it is, the Law revealed one more time.

All of a sudden the rules were revealed, and the dog owner wanted to disobey. Paul describes it this way:

> But sin, taking opportunity through the commandment [the Law], produced in me coveting of every kind; for apart from the Law sin is dead (Romans 7:8 NASB).

The Law was actually given by God to provoke sin in us. Paul states that, as a Pharisee of all Pharisees, he would not have known about coveting except through the Law. The Law actually produced in him coveting because, apart from the Law, sin is dead. The Law helps us to know that we are helpless to erase our failures. The Law was not given to us so that we could find peace with God, but to show us that we could never live up to the Law. This brings us to the next reason why God gave us His Law.

The Law Leads Us to the Cross of Jesus

The Jews of Jesus' day thought that God gave them the Law so they could save themselves through the Law. They failed with the Law! Why?

> Because they did not pursue it by faith, but as though it were by works. They stumbled over the stumbling stone (Romans 9:32 NASB).

Let's consider the following reasons as to why.

1. Their hope was set on Moses, who represented the Law.

For if you believed Moses, you would believe Me, for he wrote about Me (John 5:46 NKJV).

2. The Law was never given to be a way to salvation; salvation was given through Jesus.

So then, the law is holy, and the commandment is holy, righteous and good (Romans 7:12).

3. We were made to die once and for all to the Law through Jesus' sacrifice.

Therefore, my brethren, you also were made to die to the Law through the body of Christ, so that you might be joined to another, to Him who was raised from the dead, in order that we might bear fruit for God (Romans 7:4 NASB).

4. Now that we have died to the Law, we are completely free from the Law.

But now we have been released from the Law, having died to that by which we were bound, so that we serve in newness of the Spirit and not in oldness of the letter (Romans 7:6 NASB).

5. We have an assurance from our Father, and His promises are forever true.

For if the inheritance depends on the law, then it no longer depends on the promise; but God in His grace gave it to Abraham through a promise (Galatians 3:18).

The Law Was Given to Drive Us to Jesus

Therefore the Law has become our tutor to lead us to Christ, so that we may be justified by faith (Galatians 3:24 NASB).

The Law hasn't gone and disappeared simply because we now have Christ. The Law is still a tool God uses to draw unbelievers to Christ.

So, what was the purpose of this holy and good Law of God? Ultimately, God delivered the Law to show His creation their need for grace. They knew of His mercy (because they weren't getting what they deserved), but God wanted to reveal the power of His grace. God wanted to show them that the Law's holiness must be fulfilled and that the Lamb of God is the only one who could fulfill it.

ULTIMATELY GOD DELIVERED THE LAW TO SHOW HIS CREATION THEIR NEED FOR GRACE.

I believe this is what Jesus meant when He spoke His last words while dying on the cross, *"It is finished"* (John 19:30). Jesus fulfilled the Law for His Father, because the Law had to be completed, and none of us had the ability, or even the hope of, fulfilling the perfect and righteous Law of God.

God's task is not to fulfill the Law within believers. He has already fulfilled the Law through Christ. The Holy Spirit is not attempting to draw us into submission to the Law. The Law has been accredited to us as fulfilled!

Trying to Stop Sinning?

As I mentioned earlier, many believers have been taught and, therefore, believe that the goal of the Christian life is to quit sinning. We are obsessed with trying to stop sinning. "If I could just stop sinning, I could move in the Spirit, and then I would experience more of God."

Once again, we have misunderstood Galatians 5:16. Here is the way Galatians 5:16 is promoted far too many times. "If we will quit carrying out the desires of the flesh, then we will be walking in the Spirit."

Wrong! Notice how spiritual it sounds to tell people that if they will quit the sins that plague their lives, then and only then, will they walk in the Spirit. Here is another "miss the mark" statement: "The reason I am not experiencing God more in my life is because I have sin in my life." Or, "Because of sin, God is angry with me and has turned His back on me. If I could just stop this sin, I would be closer to God, and He would be happy with me."

The closer we look at this approach, the more we begin to see the need for performance. Remember, one of the reasons God gave the Law was to provoke sin in us. Paul boldly states:

> *But sin, taking opportunity through the commandment* [the Law], *produced in me coveting of every kind; for apart from the Law sin is dead* (Romans 7:8 NASB).

Every time we attempt to stop sinning, we end up doing the same sin over and over again, leading to frustration and shame. If we attempt to stop sinning via the Law, we will lose and never fulfill the Law, much less stop sinning. This is called "garbage can living." Let me explain garbage can living with a story.

Early one morning, the owner of a restaurant took the garbage out to the dumpster behind his restaurant. As he approached the dumpster, there was a homeless beggar digging through the garbage hoping to find morsels of food.

The owner of the restaurant said, "Hey, what are you doing in my garbage cans?"

The startled homeless beggar responded, "I am hungry. I was just looking for some food. I am out here looking for food most every day."

The restaurateur stated, "I don't want you eating out of my restaurant garbage."

The beggar became afraid as he thought the owner was angry at him for eating out of his garbage cans.

"I'm sorry, sir! I'm so hungry that I can't help myself," the beggar exclaimed.

The restaurateur said, "Hold on! I am not mad at you. I don't want you to eat from the garbage cans because I want you to eat inside my restaurant. I own this place, and I want you to eat here all the time."

"Oh, I couldn't do that," replied the beggar.

"No, I insist," said the restaurateur. "Come inside with me, and I will have my best waiter come and serve you. All of your meals will be on the house every day and any time you are hungry."

The beggar quickly stated, "But sir, I couldn't eat here all the time and certainly not for free. I might be able to eat here this time, but I am used to eating out of the garbage cans."

"Because I am the owner, I can invite you to eat here all the time," said the owner.

So the two of them went inside the restaurant. The owner seated the man at the best seat in the house. He poured the homeless man a cool glass of water and said, "Now you wait here while I go get my waiter for you."

The homeless man sat at the table thinking, *I don't deserve to be here; this is much too fancy for me.* He gazed at the beautiful cutlery, the elaborate dishes, and the fragrant flowers that adorned the table. He was amazed at the splendor of the entire restaurant.

The beggar proclaimed, "This is much too nice for me. I don't deserve this. I am not comfortable here. I think I will go back to where I am comfortable and where I am supposed to be."

So he quickly left the restaurant and returned to the garbage cans to scavenge for food.

A few minutes later, the owner checked in with his new patron only to find him gone. He walked back to the garbage area and, just as he thought, found the homeless man rummaging through the garbage.

The restaurateur passionately exclaimed, "What are you doing? I told you that you could eat for free in my restaurant all of the time. Now please, leave the garbage cans and come with me. This is where I want you to always eat. This is where you deserve to eat. Now come on, let's go. I know you are not used to eating for free, and certainly not in this kind of a beautiful restaurant, but this is all for you."

So, once again the two of them walked into the restaurant, and the owner sat the man down and left to go get the waiter.

Once again the man picked up the beautiful dishes with his dirty hands and stared at them. He looked out the back window at the garbage cans, then to the beautiful glassware and silverware, and then back to the garbage cans. Finally he said, "The owner said I was destined to eat here all the time, that I deserve it. I am so used to eating out of the garbage cans that I did not think that I deserved to eat here. I was wrong. I think I will stay right here and get used to eating in his restaurant all the time."

We are seated at the banqueting table of God. This is where we are, and we are called to remember this truth.

Many Christians experience salvation, but only momentarily believe they deserve to sit at God's banqueting table. They quickly return to the sinful lifestyle and habits that God rescued them from because they don't truly believe that they deserve anything more. Like this homeless man, many believers look at their past misdeeds and failures and compare them with God's grace and feel they are not worthy.

 ## WE WERE CREATED TO GAZE ON HIS BEAUTIFUL FACE.

But the truth is that we are not those people any more. We do not belong, metaphorically, digging through garbage cans in the alley. We belong at our King's table, not because of anything we have done, but because He has chosen us. We find our identity in His love, not in our perfect deeds. We are sons and daughters of the King, and we are seated at an abundant table. Spiritually, this is where we are, and we are called to remember this truth.

The Impossible Seems Possible

The bridal paradigm message tells us that we were created to sit at His table and to gaze on His beautiful face. We are called to renew our minds regarding who God is and who He says we are to Him. We know that our minds have been renewed when the impossible seems possible and consistent with who we really are. God wants our minds renewed so that His will can be accomplished on earth just like it is in heaven.

When we promote the idea that we should attempt to stop sinning on our own, we are set up to fail.

> *Therefore do not let sin reign in your mortal body so that you obey its lusts, and do not go on presenting the members of your body to sin as instruments of unrighteousness;* ***but present your-selves to God as those alive from the dead, and your members as instruments of righteousness to God.*** *For sin shall not be master over you, for you are not under law but under grace* (Romans 6:12-14 NASB).

All of us have had nagging sins and strongholds attempting to control us. None of us want to continue sinning; we love Jesus way too much to continue on that path. But we will be haunted by sin if we attempt to stop sinning by following the requirements of the Law. When we focus on the Law, we are actually focusing on the sin we are trying to avoid, rather than on the One who took away our sins and has promoted us to life. So place all of your fascination on Jesus and watch Him move you from sin and death into life and victory.

A Defining Story

Years ago, I heard a tragic story about a boating accident resulting in the loss of two lives. A family was enjoying a day at the lake when the father made a quick turn with the boat, and the daughter fell overboard. The father quickly turned the boat around and jumped into the water to save his daughter. The father could swim but, for some unexplained reason, he quickly drowned, leaving the little girl still thrashing about in the water. No one on board knew how to operate the boat, and it continued to drift away as the father and daughter were perishing.

Nearby, a man was fishing from a small rowboat. Seeing the accident, he began to row to the scene to help in any way he could. Paralyzed from the waist down, the man's ability to help was limited. As he approached the struggling girl, he held out an oar for her to grasp, but he could do no more because of his condition. Unable to hold on to the oar, the girl slipped beneath the surface of the water while the man watched helplessly, unable to do anything more to help her.

All of humankind is very much like the drowning girl. We are overcome by sin and unable to save ourselves. The Law of Moses, and any other system of rules, is very much like the paralyzed man attempting to rescue the girl. His intention was sincere and commendable, but he lacked the power to save the drowning girl. The Law is good, but it cannot save the sinner. Neither can the

Law release the Christian from his bondage to sin. As a matter of fact, it is the Law that somehow sustains humanity's bondage to sin. Therefore, the solution to the problem of sin is to be released from the Law and from sin.

Speaking About a Lawful Marriage

Do you not know, brothers and sisters—for I am speaking to those who know the law—that the law has authority over someone only as long as that person lives? For example, by law a married woman is bound to her husband as long as he is alive, but if her husband dies, she is released from the law that binds her to him. So then, if she has sexual relations with another man while her husband is still alive, she is called an adulteress. But if her husband dies, she is released from that law and is not an adulteress if she marries another man.

So, my brothers and sisters, you also died to the law through the body of Christ, that you might belong to another, to him who was raised from the dead, in order that we might bear fruit for God. For when we were in the realm of the flesh, the sinful passions aroused by the law were at work in us, so that we bore fruit for death. But now, by dying to what once bound us, we have been released from the law so that we serve in the new way of the Spirit, and not in the old way of the written code (Romans 7:1-6).

Death Liberates You from the Law

Romans 7:1-6 is a brilliant truth. Let's examine exactly what Paul is telling us.

Or do you not know, brethren (for I am speaking to those who know the law), that the law has jurisdiction over a person as long as he lives? (Romans 7:1 NASB).

Paul uses the phrase, *"Or do you not know"* to point out specific truths. He used this style of rhetoric in the previous chapter, as well (see Rom. 6:3,16). By using it again here, Paul is further emphasizing the truth found in Romans 7:1. Paul is simply building upon his teaching in chapter 6.

By using the term *brethren,* Paul is speaking particularly to his fellow Jewish brothers and sisters. These brethren are those who "know the law." If the Gentiles (non-Jews) are those most likely to abuse grace as an excuse for license to sin, the Jews are those who are likely to be the advocates of legalism. Jewish Christians, even the apostles, were inclined toward legalism (see Acts 10:9-18).

Paul had already made the statement, *"You are not under the law, but under grace"* (Rom. 6:14). Paul now advances this truth. How is it that Christians are no longer under the Law? They are freed from the Law by death. The Law of Moses, or other laws created by people, only apply to people while they are alive. Dead people are released from the Law.

A Hearse

When Lee Harvey Oswald assassinated President John F. Kennedy, Oswald himself was immediately assassinated outside the courtroom. Oswald was never tried because the Law only has jurisdiction over living people.

Imagine seeing a hearse speeding on its way to the cemetery and speeding through a radar trap. In pursuit, a motorcycle officer races after the hearse. When the hearse finally pulls over, the police officer does not go to the driver, but he goes to the back door of the hearse where he opens the casket and sticks the traffic ticket inside. Silly though it may be, no one can expect the Law to have authority over a dead person.

Life does look different from the vantage point of death. Paul views sanctification "from the hearse." He takes us back to the cross of Calvary—to the death, burial, and resurrection of Jesus.

Since every Christian is joined by the baptism of the Holy Spirit to Christ in His death and resurrection, Paul draws our attention to our own death in Christ. In Christ, we died to the penalty of sin. In Christ, we died to the practice of sin. In Christ, we have also died to the Law and its power over us. Our union with Christ in His death frees us from the Law.

For example, by law a married woman is bound to her husband as long as he is alive, but if her husband dies, she is released from the law that binds her to him. So then, if she has sexual relations with another man while her husband is still alive, she is called an adulteress. But if her husband dies, she is released from that law and is not an adulteress if she marries another man (Romans 7:2-3).

Paul used the analogy of marriage in these verses, but he most likely never intended to communicate a full-blown theology on marriage. Those who attempt to use Paul's analogy in this passage and expand it into a definitive statement on marriage, divorce, and remarriage are not on safe interpretative grounds.

Paul's point was simply to say that the Law of marriage applies only as long as both partners are alive. When one dies, that law is no longer applicable to the surviving partner. So let's consider what Paul intended these verses to be limited to.

Paul illustrates the principle of death making the Law null and void by comparing it to the Law's jurisdiction in marriage. Death changes all things. The death of a spouse invalidates the Law, and now a woman may remarry without violating the Law.

Therefore, my brethren, you also were made to die to the Law through the body of Christ, so that you might be joined to another, to Him who was raised from the dead, in order that we might bear fruit for God. For while we were in the flesh, the sinful passions, which were aroused by the Law, were at work in the members of our body to bear fruit for death. But now we have been released from the Law, having died to that by which we were bound, so that we serve in newness of the Spirit and not in oldness of the letter (Romans 7:4-6 NASB).

Paul communicates that we do not do anything; we don't die to the Law ourselves or kill ourselves. We were made dead to the Law through Christ's divine act. God not only delivers salvation, but also completes it. When we die to the Law, it no longer has authority over us. As believers, we are no longer married to the Law, but we are now married to Jesus Christ. This is a beautiful picture of our relationship to Christ as His Bride.

Paul is emphasizing Christ's present union with all believers. Christians identify not only with Christ's death in the past, but also with Christ in the present. In Romans 6:9, Paul declares that Christ's death was sufficient and that He will never have to die again. Those who place their faith in Jesus Christ will never lose their Bridegroom (husband) Jesus. Your marriage commitment with Christ will last forever!

A Lesson from Marriage

Let me tell you about John and Marge, a lovely married couple who lived on a sprawling estate in Atlanta, Georgia. They had been married for forty-five amazing years. While they were truly enjoying their latter days together, one spring day, John became ill and passed away shortly thereafter.

John left Marge financially well-off, and she did not have to worry about finances for the balance of her life. With the loss of John, many of her friends and family gathered around Marge, bringing her great comfort and strength.

A number of months had gone by when one of Marge's friends, Mary, came to visit. While Mary and Marge enjoyed some tea together, Mary mentioned, "You know, John left you quite wealthy. I think it would be good for you to travel to Europe. Get away, enjoy life, move on from John's death, and get a fresh start. I believe this will help you start living again."

After quite a lengthy discussion, Marge finally gave in and agreed that traveling to Europe would be nice and good for her. She thought, "Maybe a trip will help me get a fresh start."

So a few days later, she packed, hopped on a plane, and flew to Rome, Italy. She was looking forward to traveling throughout Europe to see the magnificent sights and to relax and enjoy her life again.

One sunny, beautiful day in Rome, Marge was sitting outside a quaint restaurant sipping on a cappuccino. She noticed a handsome man with tinted grey hair sitting at the table next to her. It wasn't long before he noticed Marge and was quite taken by her loveliness.

After Frank introduced himself to Marge, they discovered they were both from America. Friendly exchanges led to hours of flowing conversation. As the days went by, they continued having cappuccinos together at what was quickly becoming their favorite restaurant.

Several weeks passed, and they began to fall in love. Because of their love and desire for one another, they were married and began to travel together throughout Europe as a newly married couple. They were deeply in love.

A number of weeks passed, and they decided to return to the United States. Because Marge was a wealthy woman and Frank, as a retiree, did not have a lot of money, they decided to live in Atlanta at Marge's house.

They arrived at the Atlanta airport and took a taxi to Marge's house. As they drove up to Marge's extensive driveway, Frank was taken back by the enormous size of the historic Atlanta home. Frank commented on the beautiful pillars that framed the entrance of her lavish home. As they pulled up to the front steps, Frank paid the cab driver and whispered in Marge's ear:

"I love you. I know this is a little old-fashioned, but I would love to carry you across the threshold of our new home."

Marge loved that her new husband was so caring and excitedly agreed as Frank lifted her up. It was as if they were both in their twenties, full of excitement and anticipation of their new life together. Frank carried her into the house and set her down in the massive foyer. As he set his new bride down, he turned to close the door. As he reached for the knob, he let out a scream.

Frank frantically asked, "Marge, what is this? I mean, *who* is this?"

Frank was gazing at a huge glass case next to the front door. Inside was Marge's husband.

Frank's voice was getting louder, "Marge who is this, and what is he doing here?"

Marge calmly replied, "This is my old husband."

"What do you mean this is your old husband?" asked Frank nervously.

Marge explained, "I placed him in this glass case so I would always remember him. I could not continue living without him. Keeping him in this glass case enables me to see him daily and always remember him."

Frank yelled, "But he is dead!"

"I know," explained Marge, "but I just could not continue life without him. I had to remember him, so I had him placed in this glass case."

Frank went to the garage and found a shovel. He returned to the foyer and opened up the glass case. He removed Marge's old, dead husband and took him out to the back yard. He dug a hole and, once and for all, buried her old husband. After completing the burial he came back to Marge.

Frank explained "You need to remember that he is dead, gone, and buried and that I am your new husband, and I love you!" The significance of her husband's death finally made sense to Marge, and she lived out the rest of her life with her new husband.

As ridiculous as it sounds to keep your dead husband in a glass case in your hallway, Christians everywhere have memorialized their past in a similar way. Instead of resting in the assurance that their past life has been dead and buried with Christ, believers often remind themselves of their old, carnal life and continue to beat themselves up for their past sins.

 ## LIFE DOES LOOK DIFFERENT FROM THE VANTAGE POINT OF DEATH.

Many Christians are distracted from their true calling because they are so busy trying to ask God for forgiveness to *prove* to God that they are sorry. If God thought it necessary for us to remember our sins, he would have told us so. Instead, He told us to forget them as He has done and to leave our old-self dead and buried.

Believer, it is time for us to remember that our "old selves" are dead and gone. We need to remember that we have brand-new life in Christ.

The Purpose of the Believer's Life

The purpose of any believer's life is to glorify God by bearing fruit. This is not simply a command, but a statement of fact.

> *So, my brothers and sisters, you also died to the law through the body of Christ, that you might belong to another, to him who was raised from the dead, in order* ***that we might bear fruit for God*** (Romans 7:4).

Paul's words could literally read, "We do give fruit to God." There is no such thing as a Christian who does not bear fruit. Salvation has a product, and that product is a transformed life that bears fruit for God. Romans 6 declares that if you know Christ, you will be holy. Romans 7 states that since you are truly married to Jesus Christ, you will bring forth fruit to God.

You were once held captive by the flesh, which generated sin and led to death. But sin no longer reigns supreme in your life. Sin is no longer the master because its tyranny has been broken by Christ's death on the cross.

 ## THE TROUBLE BEGINS WHEN HE TRIES TO FULFILL THE LAW.

Is grace going to make Christians sin? No. Grace transforms believers and produces security, holiness, liberty, fruitfulness, and faith. The faith that we experience in God will not be *"in the oldness of the letter,"* but *"in newness of Spirit"* (Rom. 7:6 NASB). Our faith is not in submission to an external code or simply in a mechanical obedience to religious ritual. It cannot be an external obedience to the Law of God while the heart itself is unresponsive.

When people question God's grace by saying it leads to sin, they simply do not understand the love of God. True salvation means that God plants an entirely new nature within us. And the desire of that new nature is to know and be with God. That is why Paul said believers serve *"in newness of Spirit."* You now serve the Law better than ever because you have been redeemed. You are no longer a slave to a legal set of rules and regulations in an attempt to gain favor with God, but now you serve God out of love because He has given you salvation by His grace.

Try This Experiment

Take a tall drinking glass and place about two inches of coffee grounds in the bottom of the glass. The glass represents your soul realm, which is in the process of transformation.

Take the glass and place it under a faucet. Turn the water on slowly, barely trickling out. Allow the water to flow into the glass for a few moments. Notice that even when the water begins to flow over the top of the glass, the coffee grounds are barely leaving the glass. The slow access of water represents Sunday to Sunday living with God. Accordingly, when an individual gathers for great worship and great teaching one day per week, the presence of God's transforming power is limited.

Now, turn the water on a little stronger and allow the water to flow into the glass for a few moments. Observe that the coffee grounds are beginning to leave the glass of water, little by little. Next, turn the water on stronger and stronger and watch the flow of the water (the Holy Spirit) removing the coffee grounds.

You will begin to notice that the flowing water will move the coffee grounds out of the glass. Over time, the amount of coffee grounds in the glass will decrease. Eventually, the coffee grounds will be completely removed leaving only flowing, refreshing water in the glass.

Sometimes when believers begin to follow Christ, they focus on the coffee grounds in their lives and mistakenly see themselves as sinners. Followers of Christ need to remember that the soul realm is being redeemed, as represented by the water filling the glass (see Eph. 5:18). God does the work of transformation. We simply remember who He is and who we are to Him.

Perplexed Believers

Many believers have been perplexed by this passage from the book of Romans:

> We know that the law is spiritual; but I am unspiritual, sold as a slave to sin. I do not understand what I do. For what I want to do I do not do, but what I hate I do. And if I do what I do not want to do, I agree that the law is good. As it is, it is no longer I myself who do it, but it is sin living in me. For I know that

good itself does not dwell in me, that is, in my sinful nature. For
I have the desire to do what is good, but I cannot carry it out. For
I do not do the good I want to do, but the evil I do not want to
do—this I keep on doing. Now if I do what I do not want to do,
it is no longer I who do it, but it is sin living in me that does it. So
I find this law at work: Although I want to do good, evil is right
there with me. For in my inner being I delight in God's law; but I
see another law at work in me, waging war against the law of my
mind and making me a prisoner of the law of sin at work within
me. What a wretched man I am! Who will rescue me from this
body that is subject to death? Thanks be to God, who delivers me
through Jesus Christ our Lord! So then, I myself in my mind am
a slave to God's law, but in the sinful nature a slave to the law of
sin (Romans 7:14-25).

Paul speaks of inner turmoil. This conflict is not caused by
a selfish attitude in his heart. He is not battling against God's
Law, but he actually respects and wants to fulfill God's Law. He
states that the Law is spiritual, that the Law is good, and that
he joyfully concurs with God's Law. There is absolutely no dis-
agreement by this man with God's Law. This is something that
he agrees with and completely desires to fulfill in his spirit, mind,
will, and emotions.

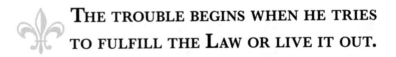

THE TROUBLE BEGINS WHEN HE TRIES
TO FULFILL THE LAW OR LIVE IT OUT.

The trouble begins when he tries to fulfill the Law or live it
out. Then he notices that everything in him rebels against his
desire to live out God's Law. This man experiences terrible inner
conflict. He desperately wants to do well (uphold the Law), but
when he tries, he utterly fails. The battle is between the members

of his body and his mind, and it makes him a prisoner of the Law of sin (see Rom. 7:23).

A question naturally arises: Is Paul speaking about a battle that is a normal Christian experience? It would be easy to believe that Paul is stating that this is a normal conflict for Christians. Many believers have stated that they feel much better knowing Brother Paul dealt with normal Christian conflict as well.

The problem is that the individual that states that he is imprisoned by his sin is the same one who also wrote, *"We are those who have died to sin, how can we live in it any longer"* (Rom. 6:2) and *"Anyone who has died has been freed from sin"* (Rom. 6:7) and *"Therefore do not let sin reign in your mortal body so that you obey its evil desires"* (Rom. 6:12).

If Paul was writing about his own experience then he would have to have spiritual schizophrenia. How can Paul be wretched and incapable of doing well one moment and the next declare freedom from condemnation and victory that can be applied to each believer?

How can Paul exhort the Philippians to rejoice (see Phil. 4:4) if he is in such turmoil? How can Paul state, *"Follow my example, as I follow the example of Christ"* (1 Cor. 11:1)? Which example are we to follow, no-way-out captivity or divine deliverance?

It is amazing that nowhere else in the New Testament do we see evidence of Paul's statements of inner conflict in Romans 7. The Apostle John, who was very close to Jesus, does not refer to any struggles that he (or we) would have with holiness. As a matter of fact, John declares just the opposite.

No one who lives in him keeps on sinning. No one who continues to sin has either seen him or known him (1 John 3:6).

No one who is born of God will continue to sin, because God's seed remains in them; they cannot go on sinning, because they have been born of God (1 John 3:9).

...for everyone born of God overcomes the world. This is the victory that has overcome the world, even our faith (1 John 5:4).

The reality for the Apostle John is not that the normal Christian experience is wrapped around an increasing sense of shame and sin consciousness. In fact, John tells us that we have God's nature in us and sin is no longer our way of life. Sin occurs in our souls on occasion, but it is not the regular way of life. If we sin, we do not have to battle; we simply repent to God through agreement with Him and thank Him for our eternal forgiveness.

What's the Conclusion?

The person in Romans 7:14-25 is under intense conviction of sin. Since the Holy Spirit has revealed the Law to him, he begins to recognize his weakness and frailty to uphold the Law. Rather than receiving grace from God, he believes that he must struggle to keep the Law in his own strength. This battle and struggle leads him to despair, frustration, bondage, condemnation, and all-out failure.

And that, my friend, is what life will look like for you when you attempt to please God by keeping the Law. Remember that one of the reasons why God gave us the Law was to provoke sin in us. In other words, every time you attempt to stop sinning via the Law, you will inevitably commit the same sin again and again with no victory, and you will experience nothing but shame and condemnation.

AREN'T YOU GLAD THAT JESUS FULFILLED THE LAW'S REQUIREMENTS FOR YOU?

Romans 7:14-25 are not verses to make you feel better about your own struggles knowing that Paul suffered likewise. They were written by Paul to show that the Law does not complete your salvation. Aren't you glad that Jesus fulfilled the Law's requirements for you? So stay married to your brand-new husband, Jesus.

Interestingly enough, Paul backs this up with his continued writings when he states in Romans 8:1 *"Therefore there is now no condemnation for those who are in Christ Jesus."*

You may be wondering, *But I still experience a battle for truth and lies. Is there a real battle? What does it look like?* In the next chapter we will look at the reality that there really is a battle for your soul. But, we have to remember where the battle is fought and what is being fought.

Summary Questions

1. Read Romans 3:20. What does the Law make us conscious of? What does the Law also reveal to us about God? (See page 129)

_____

_____

_____

_____

_____

_____

2. What does the Law provoke? (See pages 130-131.)

_____

_____

_____

_____

3. Where does the Law lead us? (See pages 131-132.)

_____

_____

_____

_____

_____

_____

4. Ultimately, God delivered the Law to show us our need for _____ (see page 133).

5. Fill in the blanks. "But _____, taking opportunity through the _____ [the Law], produced in me coveting of every kind; for apart from the _____ sin is _____" (Rom. 7:8 NASB). (See page 134.)

6. Describe what the phrase *garbage can living* means to you (see pages 134-137).

_____

_____

_____

_____

_____

_____

7. The bridal paradigm message tells us we were _____ to sit at His table and to gaze on His beautiful face (see page 137).

8. Read Romans 7:1-6. Explain what this statement means to you: Death liberates you from the Law (see pages 139-142).

_____

_____

_____

_____

_____

_____

9. Do the experiment on pages 146-147. Describe what you understand about sanctification *after* doing the experiment.

_____

_____

_____

_____

_____

_____

10. Reminder: What is the main purpose for which God gave us the Law? (See pages 150-151.)

_____

_____

_____

_____

_____

Chapter 10

Is There a Battle?

Your mind can be the gateway to hell, or it can be
the gateway to heaven.

Remember, the kingdom of God is about agreement. We either are in agreement with lies or we are in agreement with truth, and truth does set us free!

> *But I say, walk by the Spirit, and you will not carry out the* *desire of the flesh* (Galatians 5:16 NASB).

According to Paul's letter to the Galatians, we are called to walk by the Spirit (to remember who we are and who He is), and that will empower us to not carry out the desires of the flesh. I appreciate Paul reminding us to walk by the Spirit, because he reminds us of an additional reality in the next two verses: We are in a battle.

> *For the flesh sets its desire against the Spirit, and the Spirit* *against the flesh; for these are in opposition to one another, so that* *you may not do the things that you please. But if you are led by the* *Spirit, you are not under the Law* (Galatians 5:17-18 NASB).

The flesh is in direct opposition to the things of the Spirit, the things of God. Remember, the flesh is simply looking for life, but does not know where to find it. Since we are led by the Spirit (remembering who we are to Him), we will find life in that truth, and there is no law that can help find life. The Law was never given by God to help us to find life, but to reveal and convict us of sin. Paul then describes the way those living according the flesh conduct themselves:

> *Now the deeds of the flesh are evident, which are: immorality, impurity, sensuality, idolatry, sorcery, enmities, strife, jealousy, outbursts of anger, disputes, dissensions, factions, envying, drunkenness, carousing, and things like these, of which I forewarn you, just as I have forewarned you, that those who practice such things will not inherit the kingdom of God* (Galatians 5:19-21 NASB).

Paul then tells us *"...those who practice such things will not inherit the kingdom of God"* (Gal. 5:21 NASB). Wow! Is Paul serious? Does this mean that when I forget who I am and I function in the things of the flesh, such as idolatry, strife, jealousy, and outbursts of anger, I will not inherit the kingdom of God? Can I lose my salvation each time I sin and conduct myself according to the flesh?

 ## ...THIS MAKES YOU A SAINT WHO WALKS BY THE Spirit.

Paul is communicating an eternal reality. Each time you attempt to get life out of dead things, such as disputes, envying, drunkenness, and things like these, you are *currently* not walking in the Spirit. You are currently forgetting who you are, and you are not enjoying the freedom that Christ has given you. You are choosing to get your worth, value, and acceptance from things and people instead of from God. You have *not* suddenly lost your salvation, but you **are not** presently walking in the fruit of the Spirit; thus, you are not presently inheriting the kingdom of God. Paul then goes on to remind us of the fruit of the Spirit.

But the fruit of the Spirit is love, joy, peace, patience, kindness, goodness, faithfulness, gentleness, self-control; against such things there is no law. Now those who belong to Christ Jesus have crucified the flesh with its passions and desires (Galatians 5:22-24 NASB).

Paul tells us, *"Now those who belong to Christ Jesus have crucified the flesh with its passions and desires"* (Gal. 5:24 NASB). Since you have crucified the flesh, and since at one moment in time you were co-crucified with Christ (see Rom. 6:6), this makes you a saint who walks by the Spirit. The fruit of the Spirit is what you were destined for. It makes sense that someone as awesome as you are (because of Jesus) would experience the fruit of the Spirit such as love, joy, peace, patience, kindness, and all of the fruit of the kingdom.

The efforts of the flesh, simply speaking, can never give you life, because they are dead. Conversely, the fruit of the Spirit is an outgrowth of God reminding you that you are His.

Carefully consider Romans 8:14: *"For all who are being led by the Spirit of God, these are sons of God"* (NASB). Paul is telling us that we are sons of God because we have been completely redeemed by God. Those who have been redeemed by God flow in the fruit of the Spirit. So keep remembering that you are His kid!

What the Battle Looks Like

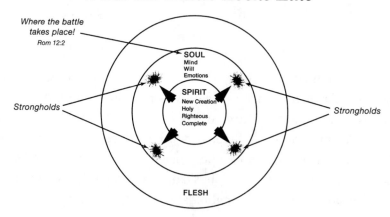

The Battle for Your Mind

According to this illustration, where is the Gettysburg? Where is the battlefield? The battlefield is in the soul realm. The mind is the battlefield: the place where our fight is won or lost. The mind is the gateway to heaven and truth; or it can also be the gateway to hell and lies.

Strongholds

Strongholds park themselves in the soul realm. Spiritually speaking, Paul defines strongholds as *"arguments and every high thing that exalts itself against the knowledge of God"* (2 Cor. 10:5 NKJV). In the previous illustration, strongholds are not destroyed by outward changes. In other words, simply changing your actions or mustering a self-generated change of actions is nothing more than self-effort or your own works. This will have no eternal effect, and transformation will not occur. God always works from the inside out. The tearing down of strongholds occurs when our spirits, the brand-new creation that God has established in us, releases victory into our souls.

STRONGHOLDS ARE ESTABLISHED THROUGH LIES, AND THEY OPERATE FROM LIES.

A stronghold is a point of operation from where Satan can keep a believer or unbeliever captive or incapacitated. A stronghold is a habitual sin or area of your life that seems to be caught in a cycle of ungodliness. Strongholds introduce shame, especially in someone who does not experience God's power to overcome the stronghold. Whether physical, emotional, psychological, or spiritual in origin, strongholds are real, and they dominate individuals. Strongholds are formed in the soul realm, are established on lies, and are strengthened solely by deception.

Signs of Strongholds

Compulsions, obsessions, fears, lusts, jealousies, violent tempers, and uncontrolled appetites of all kinds are often signs of a stronghold that is either being built or is firmly established in the soul. In most cases, the individual will recognize that something is out of control, but he or she will almost always say, "I've tried to control or stop that, but I can't seem to get on top of it."

Striking Down Strongholds

Your greatest weapons against the strongholds in your soul are intercessory worship, fasting, and exposing them to the truth! Let's take a look at an episode in the life of King Jehoshaphat, King of Israel.

> *After this, the Moabites and Ammonites with some of the Meunites came to wage war against Jehoshaphat. Some people came and told Jehoshaphat, "A vast army is coming against you from Edom, from the other side of the Dead Sea. It is already in Hazezon Tamar" (that is, En Gedi)* (2 Chronicles 20:1-2).

What did Jehoshaphat do? Like any of us, *"Jehoshaphat feared..."* (2 Chron. 20:3 NKJV). But his fear motivated him to seek the Lord, and he proclaimed a fast throughout all Judah. So Judah gathered together to ask help from the Lord, and from all the cities of Judah the people came to fast, worship, intercede, and proclaim the truth.

When we read Jehoshaphat's prayer, it ends with these words, *"We have no power against this great multitude that is coming against us; nor do we know what to do, but our eyes are upon You"* (2 Chron. 20:12 NKJV). Their eyes were solely on God, and they knew there was nothing that they could do to defeat their enemies. I am convinced that God heard their cry as they interceded, worshiped, and proclaimed the theme and truth *"...Give thanks to the LORD, for his love endures forever"* (2 Chron. 20:21).

God sent Jahaziel, a prophet to King Jehoshaphat, to assure him of the Lord's help.

Listen, all you of Judah and you inhabitants of Jerusalem, and you, King Jehoshaphat! Thus says the Lord to you, "Do not be afraid nor dismayed because of this vast armies, for the battle is not yours, but God's (2 Chronicles 20:15 NKJV).

And then Jahaziel said:

You will not need to fight in this battle. Position yourselves, stand still and see the salvation of the Lord, who is with you, O Judah and Jerusalem! Do not fear or be dismayed; tomorrow go out against them, for the Lord is with you (2 Chronicles 20:17 NKJV).

The King and the people were singing and praising before they won the victory! They knew that their God was greater than their enemy! They accepted the reality that their God was mighty, and they stood on the truth Jahaziel proclaimed to them: the battle was not theirs, it was God's.

Then we read how the enemies turned on each other and destroyed each other. King Jehoshaphat and his army did not have to lift a physical sword! The result?

The fear of God was on all the kingdoms of those countries when they heard that the Lord had fought against the enemies of Israel (2 Chronicles 20:29 NKJV).

Note what happened next, *"Then the realm of Jehoshaphat was quiet, for his God gave him rest all around"* (2 Chron. 20:30 NKJV). God can deliver us from strongholds and give us peace and spiritual rest.

It's Time to Ask God for Help!

Certain strongholds may have haunted you for many years. It is now time to ask your God for help and agree with Him and

His truth. It is okay if you are afraid (just like Jehoshaphat). As you begin to pray and ask Him for help, as you worship Him and pronounce His truth, as you meditate on His attributes, and as you fast, He will deliver you. Deliverance is His very nature.

Remember, this battle is not yours, but God's. He is simply asking you to cooperate with Him by remembering that you have the breastplate of righteousness (see Eph. 6:14) and that you are guarded on all sides with truth! You will begin to experience your faith. You will see God work in you and on your behalf. God will destroy the strongholds in your soul. It is time to stop being tormented by the flaming arrows of the enemy. Paul reminds us in Ephesians 6:14-16 to *"Stand firm,"* which means remembering to stand on the truth of God and what He has promised. Next it says, *"having girded...having put on...having shod"* (NKJV). The truths you stand on are already true about you. Paul is simply exhorting you to remember that you already have the victory. Paul tells you to *"take up the full armor of God, so that* **you will be able** *to resist in the evil day, and having done everything, to stand firm* (Eph. 6:13 NASB). This is God's promise. God will be able to deliver you from the strongholds in your soul realm! This means you are victorious!

> *Stand firm therefore, having girded your loins with truth, and having put on the breastplate of righteousness, and having shod your feet with the preparation of the gospel of peace in addition to all, taking up the shield of faith with which you will be able to extinguish all the flaming arrows of the evil one* (Ephesians 6:14-16 NASB).

Rising Above the Clouds

My good friends, Eddie and Chara Boasso, live in Kansas City, Missouri. Eddie is part of the senior leadership at the International House of Prayer in Kansas City. He agrees that the battle is between truth and lies and shared a powerful story about the battle we are in at a conference we hosted at The Prayer House in Chico, California.

Eddie told us of a time when he and Chara were leaving Kansas City International Airport. It was extremely rainy, the sky was full of dark clouds, and it looked very gloomy everywhere. As they boarded the plane, Eddie was beginning to feel the strain and oppression of the shadowy skies. As the plane began to take off, Eddie was discerning that the dark skies were a reflection of a heavy spiritual darkness over the city. He began to pray and ask for God's help.

Just as Eddie began to pray for help and proclaim God's goodness over Kansas City, the plane broke through the dark clouds. Instantly, there were clear blue skies as far as the eye could see. The sun was shining with crystal clarity and the turbulence that the plane was experiencing because of the storm clouds was gone. Eddie shared that God gave him great revelation at that moment. "It dawned on me that the sun was always shining bright and sending forth its warmth."

He added, "I had simply forgotten that the sun was always shining. I was consumed with the misrepresentation the clouds were bringing. I was only looking at the natural and not gazing on the supernatural truth that the sun was always shining."

When we are focused on what we can see in the natural realm, we will succumb to lies and experience the depression and ravage of them. But when our gaze is fixed on the always-shining light of heaven, we will walk in the truth and experience the boldness and the strength of the light. So remember, the Son of God is always shining. And, therefore, so are you!

How Do You Remain in Me?

One of my spiritual daughters, Kari Adams, shared something with me once that has stuck with me. It may help you to remember who you are while in the process of God destroying strongholds and renewing your mind.

How do you remain in Me? By making yourself constantly aware of who I am and who you are in Me.

I am God. You are My kid. I am grace. You are full of My grace. I am your provider. You are My heir. I am sovereign. You are made righteous in My sight. I am Holy. You are blameless. I am love. You are loved. Stay in the truth. Never limit your perspective to yourself, but find yourself in Me!

As we continue on our journey to discover the bridal paradigm message and all of its ramifications, it is valuable to discuss real-life issues that detain us from an abundant life with God. In the next chapter, we will tackle some of these real-life issues and explore God's remedies.

Summary Questions

1. In Galatians 5:16, how does Paul exhort us to walk? Why? (See page 155.)

_____

_____

_____

_____

_____

_____

_____

2. What is the reality Paul is reminding us about in Galatians 5:17-18? (See pages 155-156.)

_____

_____

_____

_____

_____

_____

3. How are strongholds established? (See pages 158-159.)

_____

_____

_____

_____

_____

4. List some of the common signs of a stronghold (see page 159).

_____

_____

_____

_____

_____

5. What are your greatest weapons against strongholds? (See pages 159-160.)

_____

_____

_____

_____

_____

6. How did Jehoshaphat and the armies of Israel battle their stronghold of fear? (See pages 159-160.)

_____

_____

_____

_____

_____

7. What is God's promise to you in Ephesians 6:14-16? (See page 161.)

_____

_____

_____

_____

_____

_____

Chapter 11

The Cycles

*There is a significant place of rest, and it is not
where you might think it is.*

The battle to recover from shame and manipulation while
experiencing a life full of grace and freedom is waged in two
primary areas: the renewing of your mind and the fight to believe
the truth while you are exercising your faith. This is God's process of bringing recovery from shame.

Shame is mentioned specifically in the Scriptures. When
reading the account of Adam and Eve in the book of Genesis, it
is easy to identify that they experienced shame as a result of their
sin. After they ate the fruit, they hid, tried to shift blame, and
were aware of their nakedness (see Gen. 2:25-3:10). When Adam
and Eve sinned, they introduced spiritual death and shame into
the world.

Because shame was introduced at the beginning of creation,
Paul's words to the Romans make sense and are so needed today.
"As Scripture says, 'Anyone who trusts in him will never be put to shame'"
(Rom. 10:11).

Shame is a powerful force in the lives of many believers. It has
the power to hinder us from growing into our full potential as the
Bride of Christ. Contrary to what some may believe, shame does
not just "happen," but rather is the result of systematic events that

occur outside of us, within us, and through us. To help you better understand these cycles of shame, I am going to break them down, step-by-step, so that you can identify how they might be operating in your life and how to get out of them and walk into the life that God has intended for you.

I will be referencing some material from Jeff VanVonderon's book *Tired of Trying to Measure Up*. As I mentioned previously, Jeff has been a great resource in my life concerning the subject of bridal paradigm, and his information is extremely valuable to the process of transformation. I also gleaned information from my wife, Becky, who is a clinical psychologist.

Here is an illustration that we will look at and work from.

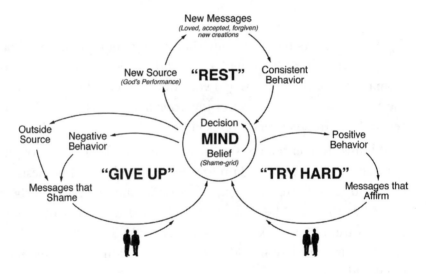

Give-Up Cycle

Let's start with the Give-Up Cycle by breaking down the characters in it. First we have outside sources, which include our parents, friends, pastors, teachers, and extended family.

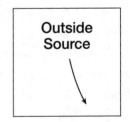

Anyone outside of yourself who speaks criticism or shame into your life can be part of this group of outside sources. These people are often simply repeating the cycle that they have been part of themselves. They have experienced criticism and shame from others, and they, in turn, are now delivering these toxic things to other people. You have simply become the recipient of their shame.

A shaming message is designed to manipulate or control the recipient. Shame messages are sometimes packaged as coded messages, comparisons, favoritism, perfectionism, rules, or rejection.

Here are some examples. As a kid, my dad would announce from the living room this coded message: "I sure wish someone would take out the garbage." Other than my parents, I was the only one in the house. From my bedroom, I had to interpret the coded message and take out the trash. I became quite good at interpreting these messages that are actually forms of shame.

Shame uses manipulation to achieve its desired results. Humiliation is a form of shame and produces utter and profound defeat. Coded messages are simply crooked speech that is designed to humiliate someone into doing something for someone else. In my case, I was humiliated into taking out the trash. In other words, the person delivering the coded message is not speaking the truth. They are simply manipulating the recipient into doing what they want. Here are more examples of shame messages:

Comparison:

"How come your sister gets A's on her report card and you can't?"

Perfectionism:

"Can't you do anything right?"

Manipulation:

"Children are to be seen and not heard."

Many individuals come from family systems where their parent(s) are addicted to drugs, alcohol, work, sex, or even religion. Many have received shaming messages from people outside their immediate families—like pastors, teachers, friends, coaches, and others. I remember receiving shame messages from my little league coach when I was a young boy. I usually struck out when I came up to bat. One time, I struck out three times in a row, and the coach yelled at me in front of the entire team—not to mention all of the people in the stands—"Winton, you are an idiot! You couldn't hit the broad side of a barn!"

Many are abused with shame from incest, spousal abuse, and child abuse. Some have received shaming messages from muggers or rapists. In nearly 60 percent of all rape cases, the victim knows their attacker. Yet, an extremely low number of victims ever report their rape. The reason is shame!

Bosses at work are outside sources and carry clout in our lives. Being passed over at work for a promotion can introduce shame and the feeling of not measuring up, as does being laid-off or fired.

Religious communities can produce shame in people when they are struggling with sin, doubting God, not complying with the leadership, not faithfully attending, not serving, or not giving financially.

Messages That Shame

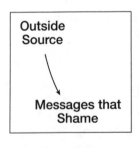

Perhaps this is the easiest part of the Give-Up Cycle to understand. Because of our ongoing experiences with outside sources, we decide who we are based upon what others say about us. When these shaming messages are delivered over and over again, they produce wounds. We translate these wounds and interpret them as: "Something is wrong with me"; "I am defective"; "I am inadequate"; "I am worthless"; "I am stupid or lazy"; or what I consider to be the worst interpretation, "I am a mistake"!

The Shame Grid: The Gateway to the Mind

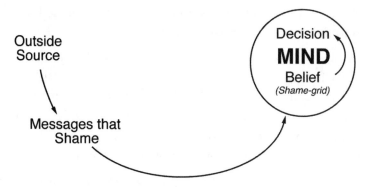

The next character to enter the Give-Up Cycle is the mind. The mind is the place where we make decisions. We also activate our emotions and our wills from our minds, which can greatly influence the decisions we make about who we think we are. At the front door of our minds is the shame grid. This shame grid has been established and fortified in us, beginning in our mothers' wombs. The shame grid continues to be formed in us as babies, and it grows with us through childhood, adolescence, and even into adulthood. The shame grid creates a belief system. In other words, what we believe about ourselves is often created through shaming messages delivered by outside sources, and it has been reinforced through the years. This belief system is forged over time, and the shame grid perpetuates a continuous cycle of shame.

The Shaming Process

Let's see this shame-driven Give-Up Cycle in action. First, you must accept that one of your outside sources is reliable and trustworthy. Often, we trust our parents, teachers, relatives, and friends as reliable sources for information about ourselves. In other words, in order for me to have the power to shame you, you have to believe that I have the power to determine the value of you as a person.

Next, you have to believe what the outside sources are saying about you, which is often the case as you have given them power in your life. Over time, as you continue to hear the same shaming messages over and over, your shame grid is formed, and you begin to agree with their assessment of you.

Finally, because of the shame grid, you become the judge and jury for who you are. You conclude that what the outside sources have said about you is true, and you condemn yourself in the courtroom of your mind. After years and years of practice, this pattern becomes normal. You never question the outside sources; you simply accept their assessment of you as factual.

Next, your will gets involved and places you at a crossroad. You either choose to "give up" or you choose to "try harder." If you conclude that your performance has failed, and you decide that you are shameful, defective, and hopeless, then you will give up. You will then choose to act in a way that agrees with your assessment of yourself.

Your Behavior

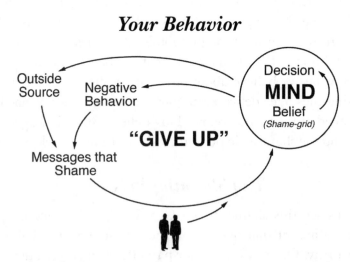

When your behavior is consistent with your shame, the cycle is nearly complete. You will typically do the exact thing that you hate to do. You do the very negative behavior that you believe lines up with the outside sources' assessment of who you are. Unfortunately, you have fulfilled the expectations of your outsides sources, because you acted just like they thought you would.

The irony is that the cycle is not complete yet. It starts over. You will continue to stay in relationships that enable you to feel as badly as you need to feel about yourself. The shame is so deeply integrated in you that you actually become the perpetrator and inflict shame on others.

For example, Martha, who lives in a marriage where her husband beats her up from time to time, encounters friends and family members who confront her.

Her friends and family members tell her:

"Are you stupid? How can you stay with that man? Don't you know that he is going to continue to do this to you? You need to leave him! Can't you see that?"

While these friends and family members truly care about Martha's physical and emotional well-being, these are shaming messages that are coming to her from outside sources that she considers reliable. She has been hearing these same messages about her husband for years, which stack on top of shaming messages she has heard about herself all of her life.

Here is the sad part of the Give-Up Cycle. Martha finally decides to call the police. Her husband is hauled away, and when he calls her from the station he says, "You know, if you had not called the police, I would not be locked up."

In other words, he is communicating to her that she is the problem and the reason that he is in jail. So she then steps back into the negative behavior and says, "I am so sorry. You're right. I will drop the charges, and we can get back together."

The reason she continues to step back into this abusive relationship with her husband is because her belief system (shame grid) has determined that someone as defective and shameful as her does not deserve to have a good relationship that is free from abuse. In other words, she deserves to be abused because she is flawed and a bad wife. She is simply acting out the behavior that agrees with her assessment of herself.

Note from the illustration that the outside sources are able to observe the negative behaviors, and this can produce more shaming messages.

They comment: "I cannot believe you are back with him"; "Have you lost your mind"; "He is such a jerk, and you're crazy to go back with him!"

Sadly, she agrees with each evaluation of her actions. This perpetuates even more sad and negative behaviors that simply agree with her assessment of herself.

Another vivid example is Beth. Beth has always had a problem with overeating. Beth grew up enjoying family BBQs. As was the custom, there was a long table covered with food including all the side dishes and desserts.

As Beth would move through the array of food, she would fill her plate. As Beth would begin to reach for the tasty deserts, Aunt Mary would say, "Beth, do you really think you need that dessert?"

Do you see the coded message? Aunt Mary was not saying what she really meant, so little Beth had to pull out her imaginary code book and decipher Aunt Mary's comment. Beth deciphered that she was fat and she should know better than to eat a piece of dessert, especially since she was fat and defective.

So the negative behavior of the Give-Up Cycle is initiated. Little Beth makes a willful decision to eat the dessert. Why? Doesn't she know that if she eats the dessert she will put on more and more weight? Yes. She is aware that she will gain more weight, but the reason Beth eats the desert is because this negative behavior agrees with her own assessment of herself. "I am defective; I am fat; no one could love me; and I am not worth anything."

Her assessment of herself is completed when she makes a final statement about herself: "I should feel badly for being such a weak person; I am such a pig." So she continues to live in the vicious cycle of overeating, and so goes the Give-Up Cycle.

The Outside Sources Re-enter

In the midst of this cycle re-enters the outside sources. The outside sources observe your behavior and shame you for it. The outside sources comment, "What's wrong with you?"; "How can you act that way?"; "You should be ashamed."; "Don't you care about yourself?"; "I am disappointed in you."

The outside sources compare you to others, or they quote Bible verses to you, almost demanding that you change. These additional shaming messages are lodged in the shame grid of your mind, further contributing to your negative belief system.

The Next Cycle: The Try-Hard Cycle

Now let's take a look at the Try-Hard Cycle. This next cycle is where many try-hard people have learned to function. They look so good on the outside because they have learned how to try really hard through self-effort.

Take John, for example, the youth pastor at a local church. On the outside, he appeared to be the ultimate youth leader to parents and teens alike. He "loved the Lord," he did daily devotions with his wife, he was available to the youth at a moment's notice, he was a musician and a worshiper, he loved to have fun, and he was a desired speaker at youth events. He looked really good! He was trying really hard.

Unfortunately, he was motivated by his own insecurity to be accepted by others. He struggled with pornography, and at times, he would drink to drunkenness. Sadly, John looked real good on the outside and received positive comments from church leaders and parents, but all the accolades could not help him. All the positive comments went into his mind, where he would tell himself, *If they really knew me, they would never say such positive comments about me. They would fire me as the youth pastor!*

Unfortunately, self-effort fails as an adequate source of inner peace and value and is no better than negative self-effort at removing shame. The goal is not to move from the Give-Up Cycle to the Try-Hard Cycle. Trying harder is not the way to break out of the Give-Up Cycle. We will discuss how to break out of both the Give-Up Cycle and the Try-Hard Cycle in our next illustration.

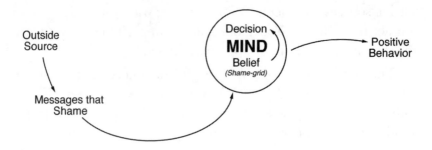

Notice what flows out of their mind and has the immediate appearance of good. When a person responds differently to the shaming messages that have barraged the shame grid and the mind, positive behaviors can now burst on the scene. Hurray! Finally, good and positive behaviors are happening! But, remember, it is possible to do all the right things for all the wrong reasons.

Let's break this down. You appear to have rejected the shaming messages that have penetrated your mind. You quickly leave the prosecutor position to become the defense attorney, determined to prove your innocence. But rejecting these messages and defending yourself against them shows that the shame messages have had their effect. Your response may be different, but the shaming wound has penetrated your thoughts and is simply producing positive behaviors for all the wrong reasons.

Serious Decisions

You make a serious decision. You are really tired of feeling badly, so you come to a different conclusion. You decide that your performance can prove that you are okay. The situation is now hopeful, and you are going to establish, once and for all, that you are a capable, determined, and powerful person. So you try harder, believing that this will work!

The Positive Behavior

Once you begin to produce positive behaviors, the Try-Hard Cycle has begun, and it will wreak havoc. You might have decided to try harder because, after an enjoyable weekend with friends, you want to try even harder to avoid the Give-Up Cycle. Or you might have just returned home from a weekend at the "National Try-Hard Conference," which was full of anecdotes and this year's flavors of really trying hard to succeed. You might be frustrated with the consequences you have experienced in the Give-Up Cycle. Or maybe you are simply fully rested up from being in the Give-Up Cycle for so long and now are really ready to try harder.

Your behavior now shifts from overeating to under-eating. If you used to neglect reading your Bible, you are now up bright and early to read your Bible. If you previously did not give money to your church, you are now proud to give money. If you deal with chemical abuse or alcohol, you grit your teeth and you abstain. And the list goes on and on.

Messages That Affirm You

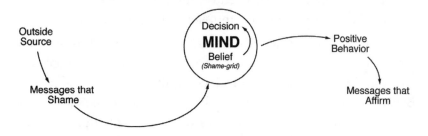

You are really doing great now that you have decided to try harder, and this has now begun to attract "messages that affirm" from the cheerleaders. They exhort you with: "You are great! See how capable you are! I knew you could do it!" Now you should feel accepted, right? But sadly you don't because these affirming messages deflect off of your shame grid as illustrated.

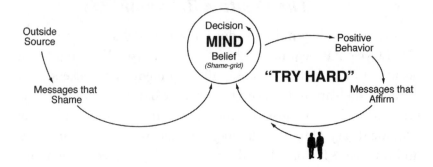

Here is where we clearly see the irony of trying to perform your way out of shame. Even as the cheerleaders encourage your performance, messages that are supposed to affirm you collide with your shame grid, and the shaming messages take over again.

Deep inside, you think to yourself: *If they really knew me, they wouldn't say those things about me. I have to keep performing so that they will continue to affirm me. I am really not as good as they say.*

In Philippians 3:1-10, Paul states that he has a habit for the things of the flesh. Paul literally says that he has a mind to place his confidence in his flesh, and he lists all the reasons why this is so natural for him. Paul, however, urges us to place no confidence in the things of the flesh because the flesh is dead. Rather, we should place our confidence and glory in Jesus Christ.

Allow me to illustrate. Bill was quite a successful businessman. He owned a growing stock brokerage firm and a mortgage company, and both companies produced quite large sums of monies. Because of his business acumen, Bill was asked to be on multiple boards within his community. Bill was a young believer and full of passion for God. Bill had been married to a wonderful woman for a number of years, and they both enjoyed their three kids. Bill was also on the board of his local church; this was quite amazing considering that he had only known Jesus for about three years.

His local church would recommend other families to him for financial counseling. He had every appearance of being the pillar of the community. Suffice it to say, Bill shined!

Multiple cheerleaders would gather around Bill with predictable comments. "Bill, you are so full of the Spirit"; "You have such wisdom"; "He is such a godly man"; "God has gifted Bill with such wisdom and the ability to make money."

However, Bill began to reject the comments coming from the cheerleaders. They actually became shame to Bill. He knew the truth about himself. Bill would make comments to himself: *If they really knew me, they wouldn't say those things about me. I have to keep performing so that they will continue to affirm me. I am really not as good as they say.*

You see, Bill had grown up in a strongly performance-driven household. Both of his parents worked, and Bill stayed home alone quite often. His father was very distant, and Bill felt he could never measure up to his dad's aspiration. Bill never remembers his dad ever saying, "I love you, son." Bill concluded that his dad loved him because he always had food on the table, and they went on family vacations every year. But what he wanted to hear the most were the words, "I love you, son. I am so proud of you."

Bill tells a story of when he was a gymnast in the eighth grade. Bill had been fairly successful as a gymnast and knew that he was going to win the outstanding athlete award at the father and son sports banquet. Bill was so excited because maybe now his dad would be proud of him.

So the big night arrived and, with a tuna casserole in hand, Bill and his dad went to the awards banquet. As Bill had expected, he won the outstanding athlete award. He thought for sure his dad would say something like, "That's great son, I am proud of you," but there was nothing! When he and his dad returned home, Bill got out of the car with the empty tuna casserole bowl. The bowl slipped out of his hands and onto the driveway, breaking into many pieces and splattering leftover tuna casserole everywhere.

His dad turned around with a look of disgust and said, "Can't you do anything right?"

Bill grew into an adult and, sad to say, he continued to perform for everyone. He was convinced that if he just tried hard enough, everyone would eventually be happy with him. So Bill carried this sad reality into his business endeavors. When business was going great, all was well; but when business would drop off, Bill would do whatever it took to increase the business, including deceiving his clientele. Performing well in front of family and friends was everything to Bill, and he would do just about anything necessary to keep it up.

At 40 years of age, Bill crashed emotionally and spiritually. Bill was exhausted from performing for the affections of all of his family and friends. Bill could not and would not stay living in the Try-Hard Cycle. After he crashed, Bill entered into counseling, and after two painful years, God gave Bill divine revelation into what God thinks of him. Bill was now experiencing healing.

Where Do We Go from Here?

If you choose to fight a behavior battle, you have two alternatives: either a negative or positive behavior. Either one of the resulting messages will produce self-effort. If you fail and give up, you are shamed, and if you try hard and succeed, you are self-righteous.

In Philippians 3:1 Paul states, *"Finally, my brothers, rejoice in the Lord! It is no trouble for me to write the same things to you again, and it is a safeguard for you."* Paul tells the church in Philippi to *"rejoice in the Lord"* one more time. Paul explains that this reminder is a *"safeguard"* for them. He was telling them this because they were forgetting who they were.

Paul continues to exhort them with this reality:

> *Watch out for those dogs, those men who do evil, those mutilators of the flesh. For it is we who are the circumcision, we who worship by the Spirit of God, who glory in Christ Jesus, and who put*

no confidence in the flesh—though I myself have reasons for such confidence... (Philippians 3:2-4).

Paul reminded them that those who were promoting an unnecessary circumcision were essentially teaching that what Jesus did was not quite enough. They were promoting self-effort, performance, and the Law.

Paul exhorted the Philippians to rejoice in the Lord because He knew that the religious leaders were urging them to rejoice in becoming great religious performers. But Paul said, "No. Boast in Jesus." In other words, Paul was urging them to rejoice in the right thing!

Some have placed their sense of value and worth in their family members or friends. While these people make great friends, sadly they will often fail us and let us down. Some boast in their cars, but your car will stop running and rust away. Some boast in their houses, others in personal possessions. Some have their lives in their bank accounts. The musical group Caedmon's Call once wrote a song that included the following words: "This world has everything / All that I could want / And nothing that I need."[1] The things of this world are all corruptible.

Ephesians 6:10 says, *"Finally be strong in the Lord, and in the strength of His might"* (NASB). The Greek word for "be strong" actually means "allow yourself to be strengthened."[2] We were created to find our strength in Jesus. It is perfectly okay with Jesus if we are weak. We find strength in Him alone, meaning we will never find strength in anything or anyone else. We were called to place all of our desires, confidence, and boasting in the unshakeable and uncreated God. He always offers eternal things worth boasting in!

You are now at a turning point in your life. Since your value and worth are no longer up for grabs, you need to learn a new cycle and depart from the old Give-Up Cycle or Try-Hard Cycle way of living. You can now place your confidence in your new source.

I hope that you can find rest and life in the midst of being His son or daughter. It's okay if you disagree with me; you can always go back to your old answers and solutions. But, I hope you won't.

Father, would You pour out wisdom and revelation into those who are reading this book. Father, may they see You and hear Your message toward them. In Jesus' name!

Introducing the Rest Cycle

In the Rest Cycle, the outside sources are still involved in our lives. And the same shaming messages are on the rampage. Unfortunately, as you begin to move into the Rest Cycle the outside sources keep delivering shaming messages that do not go away. These shaming messages still travel with sharp aim, and they first attempt to lodge and bevel their way into the shame grid of your mind.

But here is the difference. You will notice in the following illustration that the Rest Cycle begins in the middle of the old cycles, where there is no performance on your part. It begins after your last behavior and before your next behavior. It begins in the mind, the place where you believe and agree with things.

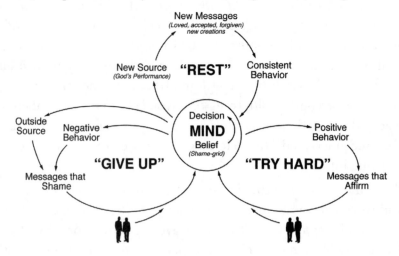

Let's Meet the Characters

God's character and the gift of His salvation absolutely contradict and obliterate everything in the shame message that says you are defective, unworthy, unloved, or unaccepted. Instead of the normal outside sources, you now have a brand-new source. God has now become the irrefutable source of all truth messages about you. God stands declaring His thoughts and emotions about you to you—a wounded and hurting person. His posture is one of compassion, grace, and complete forgiveness. Even though you are faced with outside sources that continue to shame you, you have a new source who brags about you. He is the great healer of all emotions in your soul. You are His, and no one can steal you away from Him.

God sent His Son for you because He loves you. And because He sent His Son for you, His Holy Spirit is now dwelling in you. He will dwell with you always and forevermore! His presence in you is the one constant in a turbulent and noisy world. The Holy Spirit is called the Comforter and Helper because we are all in need of comfort and help.

All of your guilt is gone through Jesus' sacrifice. The penalty that you would have to pay has been paid in full. You have been rescued from death, and life is now yours. It is all about Jesus' ultimate death and resurrection. What a new source you have!

The new source has released a new message about you that is eternal! You are completely and utterly loved and accepted. You are fully loveable and fully acceptable! God actually enjoys you! Any laws you tried to keep would not have achieved this. You are a brand-new creation—clean, fresh, whole, lacking in nothing. You are now His heir. It is now time to agree and remember the truth of who you are. Peter clearly reminds us to keep remembering who we are.

So I will always remind you of these things, even though you know them and are firmly established in the truth you now have. I think it is right to refresh your memory as long as I live in the tent of this body, because I know that I will soon put it aside, as our Lord Jesus Christ has made clear to me. And I will make every effort to see that after my departure you will always be able to remember these things (2 Peter 1:12-15).

Therefore, your fight is no longer based on the need to produce good enough behaviors, but is characterized by believing what is true about you according to what God says and has done. When you agree with the truth that God declares over your life, you will begin to see consistent behaviors.

Consistent Behaviors

Your behavior is now consistently aligning with the message of what God has said about you. Now your behaviors are experiencing the process of transformation.

Look at the following illustration. Where do the arrows go from consistent behavior? They go into the mind, causing deeper transformation.

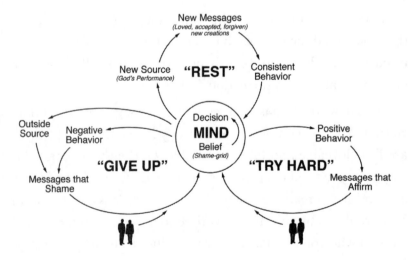

This process *is* the renewing of your mind. Paul emphasizes this in Romans 12:2:

> Do not conform any longer to the pattern of this world, **but be transformed by the renewing of your mind.** Then you will be able to test and approve what God's will is— his good, pleasing and perfect will.

You have a new way of thinking, processing, and choosing life. Paul speaks in Galatians 5:25, *"If we live by the Spirit, let us also walk by the Spirit"* (NASB). In other words, if God's Spirit is now your source from which you get life, then continue to walk this way.

The Rest Cycle at Work

The following are some scenarios that show the Rest Cycle in action.

Scenario 1: John

John has been a diligent and hard worker. He is anticipating a promotion and a raise at work. But John discovers that someone else in the company has received the promotion and raise.

Reaction Guided by Performance-Based Thinking

The Problem: This really hurt me, and I closed myself off to my boss and everyone I work with.

The Emotion: I felt like a child sent to his room because I made a serious mistake.

The Shaming Message: If I were a better worker, I would have been promoted.

The Shaming Conclusion: I must be incapable. I am not a good worker. I give up.

Response Guided by God-Based Thinking

God as the Source: God is my source for all things, including my job.

God's New Message: God says I am good enough, and even though I was passed up for the job, I know my value and worth are not derived from what I do, but rather who I am and whose I am.

The Consistent Behavior: I can walk out of my office and interact with my fellow employees and my boss. God loves me, and I am fully accepted by Him, no matter the position I hold at work.

Scenario 2: Nathaniel

Nathaniel grew up in a strongly shame-based family. His mother was constantly berating him by making statements such as, "Can't you do anything right?" "You have such a big nose." "You need to apologize to Uncle Frank because you were judgmental to him." "Children need to respect their elders." Years later, Nathaniel's parents came to visit him and his wife, and his mother continued to call him judgmental. According to his mother, everything Nathaniel did or said was judgmental.

Reaction Guided by Performance-Based Thinking

The Problem: This has been going on all my life; maybe my mother is right. I must be judgmental. God must view me as a judgmental person.

The Emotion: I feel like a judgmental and negative person, and I need to change my attitude. God does not accept me because I am judgmental.

The Shaming Message: If I were a nonjudgmental person, my mother would respect me, and we would get along. The Lord would be proud of me and receive me because I would be acting graciously.

The Shaming Conclusion: I am not a good person, and I need to shape up and try harder.

Response Guided by God-Based Thinking

God as the Source: God is my source for all things, including my relationship with my mother.

God's New Message: God says I am His. I am approved and accepted by God. I am safe with Him. I am His son who is fully capable of loving all people. The truth is that I am not judgmental, but that I see things through His eyes, which are full of grace and mercy.

Consistent Behavior: I can interact with my family, knowing that I am loved and accepted and fully able to love others.

Scenario 3: Mary

Mary struggles with relationships. She often finds herself dating men who put her down and treat her like a tramp. Her children and friends do not like the men she dates nor do they want them to attend any family events. Mary struggles to end her relationship with a man for fear of being alone.

Reaction Guided by Performance-Based Thinking

The Problem: Someone is always mad at me. My friends and family complain I do not have enough time with them. My boyfriend also complains I do not spend enough time with him.

The Emotion: I fear I will have to choose between my family, my friends, and my boyfriend.

The Shaming Message: It is my job to make everyone in my life happy, no matter what it takes.

The Shaming Conclusion: I am so tired, but I must become better at making everyone around me happy and content with me.

Response Guided by God-Based Thinking

God as the Source: God is my source in the midst of all my relationships.

God's New Message: God is my ultimate relationship, and with Him there are no strings attached. I am safe with Him even if I don't have a boyfriend. God says I am full of His Spirit and capable of good and healthy relationships.

The Consistent Behavior: I can enjoy positive male relationships. I do not have to settle for men who treat me poorly. I can also enjoy relationships with my friends and family. I do not have to keep trying to make everyone happy.

Scenario 4: Susan

When Susan was a young woman, her friend's father abused her for four years. As an adult, she struggles to be emotionally and sexually intimate with her husband.

Reaction Guided by Performance-Based Thinking

The Problem: I struggle to be intimate with my husband and often try to avoid any overtures of intimacy.

The Emotion: I become frightened as my husband has sex with me, and I often feel as if my abuser is raping me again.

The Shaming Message: If I were a better wife, I would not have this reaction. I should get over this and enjoy my husband.

The Shaming Conclusion: I am defective. Something is wrong with me. Our relationship will never get better.

Response Guided by God-Based Thinking

God as the Source: I am loved and created by God. He is my source. God takes good care of me and my emotions.

God's New Message: God says I am His. I am loved and fully accepted into His heart. I am safe with Him. He will help me feel safe with my husband.

The Consistent Behavior: I can enjoy intimacy with my husband. God has redeemed my past and will support my desire to have an intimate relationship with my husband. I no longer have to "give up"; God's love for me is enough.

God has Provided a Way

God loves for us to step into Him. As we do, He will provide a way of escape from the arduous lies of the enemy. I have seen the results from the Rest Cycle in my own life and in the lives of countless others. I believe God has given this tool as a means of escape from the demanding lies of the Give-Up Cycle and the Try-Hard Cycle. Paul articulates this kingdom reality in First Corinthians 10:13:

*No temptation has overtaken you except what is common to mankind. And God is faithful; he will not let you be tempted beyond what you can bear. But when you are tempted, **he will also provide a way out** so that you can endure it.*

The way out of the Give-Up Cycle and the Try-Hard Cycle is the Rest Cycle. Through the Rest Cycle, you will discover the bridal paradigm reality and His eternal message that you are His and that God is your source. Ask Him to help you process through this cycle, and watch Him move your emotions, will, and mind into behaviors that are consistent with who you really are!

I remind you that God has not abandoned you to figure out how to heal yourself. In the next chapter, we will take a look at an additional and timeless tool God has given to each of us to overcome both the Give-Up Cycle and the Try-Hard Cycle. This enduring tool has been forgotten, and very few individuals exercise this tool. If you will embrace this tool, you will hear the Father's heart pounding toward you!

Summary Questions

1. What are the two primary areas of the battle to recover from shame and manipulation? (See page 167)

_____

_____

_____

_____

_____

2. *"As Scripture says, 'Anyone who trusts in* _____ *will never be put to* _____ *'"* (Rom. 10:11). (See page 167.)

3. A shaming message is designed to _____ or _____ the recipient (see page 169).

4. According to the Give-Up Cycle, list some examples of outside sources in *your* life (see page 168).

_____

_____

_____

_____

_____

_____

5. What shaming messages did you receive from outside sources?

_____

_____

_____

_____

_____

6. The shame grid is the establishment of a belief system that determines what you believe about yourself. How does the shame grid perpetuate shame? (See page 171.)

_____

_____

_____

_____

_____

7. Describe the shaming process in the Give-Up Cycle (see pages 171-172).

_____

_____

_____

_____

_____

_____

8. What are negative behaviors? Why do negative behaviors occur? (See pages 172-175.)

_____

_____

_____

_____

_____

9. Who are cheerleaders, and what is their role in the Try-Hard Cycle? (See pages 177-178.)

_____

_____

_____

_____

_____

10. Are there outside sources and shaming messages in the Try-Hard Cycle? (Circle one)Yes No

11. True or False: Do the messages from the outside sources in the Try-Hard Cycle go through the shame grid?

12. Are positive or negative behaviors generated in the Try-Hard Cycle?

_____

_____

13. Where are positive behaviors generated? (See pages 177-178.)

_____

_____

_____

_____

_____

_____

14. Why are positive behaviors not necessarily good? (See pages
    177-178.)

_____

_____

_____

_____

_____

15. Where do the cheerleader comments in the Try-Hard Cycle
    go? (See pages 178-182.)

_____

_____

_____

_____

_____

16. The outside sources and shaming messages don't go away
    simply because you have entered the Rest Cycle. So, where
    does the Rest Cycle begin? (See page 182.)

_____

_____

_____

_____

_____

17. Who is our source in the Rest Cycle? (See page 182-184.)

_____

_____

_____

_____

_____

_____

18. What message does our new source give us? (See page 182-184.)

_____

_____

_____

_____

_____

_____

19. Your behavior is now consistently aligning with the _____ of what God has said about you. Now your behaviors are experiencing the process of _____ (see page 184).

20. Write out Romans 12:2.

_____

_____

_____

_____

_____

_____

21. In light of the Rest Cycle, what is your interpretation of First Corinthians 10:13?

_____

_____

Endnotes

1. Caedmon's Call, "This World," *Chronicles 1992-2004* (Essential Records, 2004), track 5; lyrics available at http://www.metrolyrics.com/this-world-lyrics-caedmons-call.html (accessed February 17, 2012).

2. Thayer and Smith, *The KJV New Testament Greek Lexicon*, s.v. "Edunamoo" (#1743); BibleStudyTools.com; http://www.biblestudytools.com/lexicons/greek/kjv/endunamoo.html (accessed February 17, 2012).

Chapter 12

God Gives Tools

*When we become consumed with God, there is
nothing more rewarding than meditating on Him.*

G od does not give the Church things; He gives the Church His
Son Jesus. God not only "gave' His Son to each of us, but
He has also given tools to each of us so that we can discover fresh
wisdom and revelation of His Son.

Do you know why the Word of God is true? Because it is true!
God cannot and does not lie! Titus speaks this truth:

> *...knowledge of the truth that leads to godliness—in the hope of
> eternal life, which God, **who does not lie**, promised before
> the beginning of time* (Titus 1:1-2).

God makes eternal promises, and there is nothing more profound than the promises of a God who never lies. You can trust
every word that He has spoken. Meditation is by far one of the
most important life principles we can ever learn. God's Word is
His true and eternal thoughts written on paper for our study and
consideration. His Word is how He thinks about every situation
and subject.

WE BECOME LIKE THE THING WE

FOCUS ON.

Do not be afraid of meditation because it sounds like it is part of the New Age movement. Satan is the great imposter. He has never created anything. He will introduce his own thoughts (which are all lies) and twist them from God's original intent. Satan will not only twist what God is doing by perverting it (New Age meditation), but he will keep well-meaning believers from experiencing these powerful tools out of fear. Some believers are convinced that meditation is only an apparatus of the New Age movement.

God says to meditate on His Word day and night so we will obey it (see Josh. 1:8). The psalmist says, his delight is in the Law of the Lord, and in His Law he meditates day and night (see Ps. 1:2). Actually, the Bible mentions *meditate* or *meditation* twenty times. My encouragement and my exhortation to you is to meditate on the Word of God—*not* with the goal of finishing, but with the goal of being with Him! In other words, don't feel like you have to finish a particular passage of Scripture during your meditation. If you find yourself completely absorbed in meditating on the first verse of a passage, and that is all you meditate on, then you have accomplished your longing of meeting with Him.

The Beauty of Meditation

Meditating on God's Word is an extremely valuable tool in your identity. We take on the attributes of the things we focus on. When we become consumed with God, there is nothing more rewarding than meditating on Him. I am intrigued with David's thoughts as he meditated on God and penned this psalm:

> *The Lord is my light and my salvation; Whom shall I fear? The Lord is the defense of my life; Whom shall I dread? When evildoers came upon me to devour my flesh, my adversaries and my enemies, they stumbled and fell. Though a host encamps against me, my heart will not fear; though wars arise against me, In spite of this I shall be confident* (Psalm 27:1-3 NASB).

In verse 1, David professes and agrees that God is his light and salvation. When he understands and agrees with this truth, he fears no one and nothing. When David does *not* remember who God is (his light and salvation), he then agrees with fear.

This really drives home the truth that God's perfect love casts out all fear (see 1 John 4:18). When you are experiencing fear, you are not experiencing His light. When you are *not* drawing your life from God, you are walking in the darkness. Darkness is simply the absence of light. When God is welcomed in and steps into the darkness, the darkness leaves, because the light of God is present and all fear is gone.

Next, David believes that God is the great defender of his life, and because of this reality, he dreads no one. This means that Jesus defends David (and you) in the courtroom of all eternity. Lies from the enemy are toothless.

In verse 2, David comments that when we remember who God is, and who we are, our enemies will stumble and fall. In other words, darkness has no power when we remember who God is and who He says we are. In reality, darkness is a lie. Even when my enemies attempt to come back again and again, they are revealed by God's light and they vanish. And with this reality, my heart will not fear; I will be secure in God!

> One thing I have asked from the Lord, that I shall seek: that I may dwell in the house of the Lord all the days of my life, to behold the beauty of the Lord and to meditate in His temple (Psalm 27:4 NASB).

In Psalm 27:4, I am struck by what David *did not* say: "Lord there are ten really important items in my life, but you are the most important item in my life." He actually stated that nothing else in his life mattered. Jesus, and Jesus alone, is my passion and my desire. He is my fascination. His transcendent beauty is all that I will gaze on. In other words, nothing else matters when I have Him, because in Him I have all things.

Supernatural revelation is released from God's realm when we meditate on His very thoughts and intentions. An incredible obsession for the kingdom of heaven occurs when we meditate on the Beautiful One. This verse will be familiar to many, *"But seek first His kingdom and His righteousness, and all these things will be added to you"* (Matt. 6:33 NASB). As we meditate on Him, His presence will increase in our hearts. To behold God is to know God.

The Song of All Songs

I would like to encourage you to meditate on passages such as this:

> *Let him kiss me with the kisses of his mouth—for your love is more delightful than wine. Pleasing is the fragrance of your perfumes; your name is like perfume poured out. No wonder the maidens love you! Take me away with you—let us hurry! Let the king bring me into his chambers* (Song of Solomon 1:2-4).

Song of Solomon illustrates the Bride's spiritual journey as she draws near to Jesus in intimacy and then runs in deep partnership with Him in ministry. She matures in these two realities as she experiences the intimacy of God's Word touching her heart. The paradox of our faith is that we are dark in our souls, yet we are lovely to God. God has the divine perspective of the finished Bride, complete and holy. Both truths must be held in tension to understand who we are before God.

WE ARE LOVELY TO GOD.

Some emphasize how sinful we are, and others emphasize how beautiful we are. While we need to understand that we sin and forget who we are, the deeper revelation is that we are beautiful, powerful, and lovely to God. There is nothing we can do to make God love us more, and there is nothing we can do to lose His love for us.

The Bride has a desperate cry to have more of Jesus. She wants Him to personally feed her spirit.

Tell me, O You whom I love, where You feed your flock...For why should I be as one who veils herself by the flocks of Your companions? (Song of Solomon 1:7 NKJV)

Mike Bickle, director of the International House of Prayer in Kansas City, teaches that there are four reasons why God is passionate toward us, even in our weakness.

1. God's personality is filled with tender and loving emotions for His people.

2. With the gift of righteousness, we also freely receive the beauty of Jesus' righteousness.

   For He made Him who knew no sin to be sin for us, that we might become the righteousness of God in Him (2 Corinthians 5:21 NKJV).

3. The Spirit imparts a sincere and willing spirit of obedience that cries for God; it is not a fully mature obedience, but it is a very willing spirit of obedience.

   ...You received the Spirit of adoption by whom we cry out, "Abba, Father" (Romans 8:15 NKJV).

4. We have an eternal destiny as Jesus' Bride. God sees the end from the beginning. He sees us as the finished Bride.[1]

Let Me Illustrate

Kirk Bennett, also from the International House of Prayer, tells a beautiful story that affirms the power of meditating on God's Word.

Once, after he taught about meditating on the Word of God, a young woman (we will call her Mary) came up to Kirk. She was so excited about beginning her journey of meditating on God. Mary said that God had really ignited her heart toward meditation, and she was looking forward to the process.

About three weeks later, Kirk was walking in the halls, and he noticed Mary was walking briskly toward him. As she got closer and closer to him, she was beginning to bounce and dance. Mary was so filled with the Spirit. Mary's smile was so contagious, and her eyes were beaming with joy.

Kirk said, "Wow! What is going on with you?"

Mary began to tell Kirk that she had spent the past three weeks meditating on the Word of God.

Kirk responded, "That's awesome! What verses have you been meditating on?"

Mary said, "John 3:16!"

Kirk said, "That's so cool. What part of John 3:16 have you been meditating on?"

Mary said with much exhilaration—"For God!"

Mary had spent three weeks on only two words from John 3:16, and she had found such deep revelation from God. The point is not to be in a rush. The goal of meditation is not to finish, but to be with the One who loves you. God has such divine revelation that He wants to give us, and this revelation can even be found in only two words from Scripture. The truth is that we can be intimate with a beautiful and completely unfathomable God.

> *...whatever is true, whatever is honorable, whatever is right, whatever is pure, whatever is lovely, whatever is of good repute, if there is any excellence and if anything worthy of praise, dwell* [meditate] *on these things* (Philippians 4:8 NASB).

> *Let the word of Christ richly dwell **[live]** within you, with all wisdom teaching and admonishing one another with psalms and*

hymns and spiritual songs, singing with thankfulness in your hearts to God (Colossians 3:16 NASB).

Here are some Scriptures you can meditate on. And remember, God does not lie (see Titus 1:2).

Who Am I According to God?

Matt. 5:13: I am the salt of the earth.

Matt. 5:14: I am the light of the world.

John 1:12: I am a child of God.

John 15:1,5: I am part of the true vine, a channel (branch) of His (Christ's) life.

John 15:15: I am Christ's friend.

John 15:16: I am chosen and appointed by Christ to bear His fruit.

Rom. 6:18: I am a slave of righteousness.

Rom. 6:22: I am enslaved to God.

Rom. 8:14-15: I am a child of God.

Rom. 8:17: I am a joint heir with Christ, sharing His inheritance with Him.

1 Cor. 3:16; 6:19: I am a temple of God. His Spirit dwells in me.

1 Cor. 6:17: I am joined to the Lord and am one spirit with Him.

1 Cor. 12:27: I am a member of Christ's body.

2 Cor. 5:17: I am a new creation.

Gal. 3:26,28: I am a child of God and one in Christ.

Gal. 4:6-7: I am an heir of God since I am a child of God.

Eph. 1:1: I am a saint.

Eph. 3:1; 4:1: I am a prisoner of Christ.

Eph. 4:24: I am righteous and holy.

Col. 3:3: I am hidden with Christ in God.

Col. 3:4: I am an expression of the life of Christ because He is my life.

Col. 3:12: I am chosen of God, holy, and dearly loved.

1 Thess. 1:4: I am chosen and dearly loved by God.

1 Thess. 5:5: I am a child of light and not of darkness.

Heb. 3:1: I am a holy brother, partaker of a heavenly calling.

Heb. 3:14: I am a partaker of Christ; I share His life.

1 Pet. 2:5: I am one of God's living stones and am being built up as a spiritual house.

1 Pet. 2:9-10: I am a chosen race, a royal priesthood, a holy nation, a people for God's own possession to proclaim the excellencies of Him.

1 Pet. 2:11: I am an alien and stranger to this world I temporarily live in.

1 Pet. 5:8: I am an enemy of the devil.

1 John 3:1-2: I am now a child of God. I will resemble Christ when He returns.

By the Grace of God I...

Rom. 5:1: Have been justified.

Rom. 6:1-6: Died with Christ and died to the power of sin's rule over my life.

Rom. 8:1: Am free forever from condemnation.

1 Cor. 1:30: Have been placed into Christ by God's doing.

1 Cor. 2:12: Have received the Spirit of God into my life that I might know the things freely given to me by God.

1 Cor. 2:16: Have been given the mind of Christ.

1 Cor. 6:19-20: Have been bought with a price. I am not my own. I belong to God.

2 Cor. 1:21: Have been established, anointed, and sealed by God in Christ.

Eph. 1:13-14: Have received the Holy Spirit, who was given to me as a pledge guaranteeing my inheritance to come.

Eph. 1:4: Have been chosen in Christ before the foundation of the world to be holy and without blame before Him.

Eph. 1:5: Was predestined to be adopted as a child.

Eph. 1:7-8: Have been redeemed and forgiven and am a recipient of His lavish grace.

Eph. 2:5: Have been made alive together with Christ.

Eph. 2:6: Have been raised up and seated with Christ in the heavenlies.

Eph. 2:18: Have direct access to God through the Spirit.

Eph. 3:12: May approach God with boldness, freedom, and confidence.

Col. 1:12-13: Have been delivered from the domain of darkness and transferred to the kingdom of Christ.

Col. 1:14: Have been redeemed and forgiven of all my sins.

Col. 1:27: Have Christ Himself within me.

Col. 2:7: Have been firmly rooted in Christ and am now being built up in Him.

Col. 2:11: Have been spiritually circumcised (the old me is dead and gone).

Col. 2:10: Have been made complete in Christ.

Col. 2:12-13: Have been buried, raised, and made alive in Christ.

Col. 3:1-4: Have been raised up with Christ. I died with Christ. My life is now hidden with Christ in God. Christ is now my life.

2 Tim. 1:7: Have been given a Spirit of power, love, and a sound mind.

2 Tim. 1:9: Have been saved and called (set apart) according to God's doing.

Heb. 2:11: Am sanctified and am one with the sanctifier; therefore, He is not ashamed to call me His sibling.

Heb. 4:16: Have a right to come bodily before the throne of God to find mercy and grace in times of need.

Summary Questions

1. What is released when we meditate on Scripture and learn God's thoughts and intentions? (See pages 197-198.)

_____

_____

_____

_____

_____

_____

_____

2. God says to _____ on His Word day and night so we will _____ it (see Josh. 1:8; Ps. 1:2). (See page 198.)

3. The goal and passion of every believer is not to finish a passage of Scripture while meditating, but to ___ _____ ____ (see page 198).

4. _____ _____ is released from God's realm when we meditate on His thoughts and intentions (see page 200).

5. What are some reasons why God is passionate toward us, even in our weakness? (See pages 200-201.)

_____

_____

_____

_____

_____

_____

Endnote

1. Mike Bickle, "Studies in the Song of Solomon: Progression of Holy Passion," notes (Kansas City, MI: Forerunner School of Ministry, 2007), 49.

Chapter 13

God Believes in You

He gave Himself to you because He loves you and He desires for you to partner with Him in recapturing the earth for His namesake!

God has plenty to say about you. One of the greatest messages in all of Scripture, speaking of us as the Bride to Jesus, is the bridal paradigm message from Song of Solomon 1:15. *"How beautiful you are, my darling! Oh, how beautiful! Your eyes are doves."*

Jesus declares that we have "dove eyes." A fascinating aspect of doves is that they are single-minded; a dove has no peripheral vision. It only sees straight ahead. It is not distracted by what is happening at its right or left. An additional aspect of doves is that they are very loyal. A dove will mate once in its life. If its mate dies, it never mates again. This speaks symbolically of loyalty. God claims this about you! To Him you are focused on Him and Him alone, and you are loyal. Your commitment to Him as a voluntary lover is sealed. The revelation of being loved and beautiful to God is to see with dove's eyes. God's eternal message to each of us is that we are glorious and full of power to Him.

The Old Man and His Son

An old man and his beloved son lived together in a beautiful home. Their home was adorned with priceless paintings that would fetch millions of dollars. They hosted paintings from some of the most famous painters in history—Pablo Picasso, Vincent Van Gogh, Georgia O'Keefe, and many others. The man and his son had a great love for these paintings, and they would sit around the house admiring these priceless works of art on a daily basis.

One spring day, the son was drafted by their nation's military. While the father would miss his son, he was very proud of him. Early in December, the father received word from the military that his son had died serving his country. Additional word came that the enemy had killed his son as he rescued men from the front line. His life was given for the lives of his comrades.

One day shortly before Christmas, as the father was sitting in the living room flanked by his priceless array of paintings, he began to weep. The father knew he would never again be with his son, and they would never celebrate Christmas together again.

Later, there was a knock at the door. When the father opened the door, a tall, slender young man stood at the doorway. The young man introduced himself as one of his son's military friends. The father invited the young man in and noticed the young man carrying a rather large, wrapped package. As the father and the young man were enjoying a cup of tea, the visitor told the father that he was one of the survivors his son had given his life for.

The young man added, "As a matter of fact, your son saved multiple lives; his life was not given in vain. I brought this gift for you in remembrance of your son. I am a painter and a great lover of art, and your son shared that you both loved art."

As the father opened the package, it revealed a stunning painting of his son's face. The likeness was striking. The young man told the father that he was not the best painter, but that his son had meant everything to him.

The father commented, "This painting is glorious, and I thank you from the bottom of my heart. This means everything to me, and I will display it with love and honor."

As the father and the young man finished their time together, and after an emotional goodbye, the father placed the painting of his son in the most prominent place in the house. He removed the most valuable and famous of the paintings from above the fireplace and hung the painting of his son there instead. This was now his most prized painting.

Shortly after the first of the year, the father took ill and passed away. Art collectors from all over the world were eager because the man had no other heirs, and these priceless works of art would now be auctioned off. Art dealers from around the world were ecstatic.

The day of the auction finally arrived, and the auction room was full of buzz. Finally these art collectors would have opportunity to bid on these fine works of art.

As the auction began, the auctioneer lifted up the first piece of art to be bid on. All of the art collectors realized that this was not one of the famous pieces.

Someone in the crowd shouted out, "What is this painting? What is this? This is not what we have come to bid on!"

The auctioneer moved out onto the auction floor and replied: "Who will bid on this piece of art?"

There was no response.

The auctioneer repeated, "Who will bid on this piece of art?"

The auctioneer continued, "Who will give $100.00 for this piece of art?"

Still there was no response.

The auctioneer stated, "Who will give me $75.00?"

Still, there was no response.

The auctioneer was stunned, but said, "Who will give me $50.00?"

The crowd was stirring with wonderment.

Then a shout from the crowd came, "Why this painting first?"

Finally someone in the crowd shouted out, "I know who the subject of that painting is. That is the owner's son who died in the war."

All of the art collectors were stunned and remained silent for a few moments.

The man who recognized the painting shouted out, "I only have $10.00 for the painting, will you take that?"

The auctioneer shouted, "Will anyone go higher?" The auctioneer waited a moment before he said, "Going once. Going twice. Sold to this man for $10.00."

Then the auctioneer calmly stated: "The auction is now over."

Bellows could be heard throughout the auction hall.

"Hey! We did not come here to purchase some cheap painting!"

Others clamored: "There are millions of dollars of paintings yet to be auctioned! What do you mean the auction is now over?"

The auctioneer replied: "It's simple. According to the father's will, whoever takes the portrait of the son gets it all!"

My friend, if you have received Jesus' eternal love for you and have been redeemed, then you get it all.

We Get It All

God believes in you so much that you get the entire kingdom because you are His beloved child. You have received Jesus' eternal sacrifice. He gave Himself to you because He loves you, and He desires you to partner with Him in recapturing the earth for His namesake! Our Father has placed you at His banqueting table. All of the gifts are resident at the banqueting table: all the anointing, power, and strength of heaven. There is hope, purpose for life, water that will never let you be thirsty again, and eternal food that will sustain you; in fact, the entire kingdom of God is resident at the table of God.

ALL OF THE GIFTS ARE RESIDENT AT THE BANQUETING TABLE.

After hearing the bridal paradigm teaching multiple times, Kari, a leader at the Chico YWAM Discipleship Training School, said:

"Ken, each time I hear you teach bridal paradigm I am re-energized and reminded one more time that I am His beloved. But every time you begin to teach the banqueting table part of the bridal paradigm, I get a little confused."

I replied, "What is it that is confusing?"

Kari said, "Well, all of your teaching is right from Scripture, and it tells me that I am already holy and that I am already and always will be at the banqueting table. Yet, you teach that we need to remember who we are, and if we forget who we are, we need to come back to the banqueting table."

I responded, "Well, yes, that is true."

Kari said, "No. That is not true."

This of course provided me with a great moment to remember who I am. Kari was challenging the teacher!

I carefully said, "Kari, tell me how my teaching is not true concerning the banqueting table?"

Kari gently stated, "Well, if I am already holy, righteous, redeemed, a saint, and a new creation, then I am always at the banqueting table. The new me—my new spirit, who you and the Scriptures say that I am—is always at the banqueting table. You need to remind people that they are already, and always will be, there! We just need to remember this truth!"

I said, "Wow! You are right. We are always there; we simply forget that we are there. It's like when we sin; we simply forgot who we are, and we need to remember that we are always His saints and that we are always at His table."

So God gave the both of us fresh revelation on who we are and where we reside!

Scripture backs up the banqueting table reality:

For our citizenship is in heaven, from which also we eagerly wait for a Savior, the Lord Jesus Christ (Philippians 3:20 NKJV).

We are citizens of heaven; our home is now and forever in heaven. As a matter of fact, Scripture tells us that we are currently seated in heavenly places.

*...and raised **us** up with Him, and seated **us** with Him in the **heavenly places** in Christ Jesus* (Ephesians 2:6 NASB).

As citizens of heaven, we are not battling to get back into a place that we already are. We simply forgot that we were already there.

God Really Does Believe in You

Did you know that God believes in you? Do you know why God uses flawed and weak people? Because we are all He has! Let's see if God believes in you according to Scripture.

Jesus went throughout Galilee, teaching in their synagogues, preaching the good news of the kingdom, and healing every disease and sickness among the people. News about him spread all over Syria, and people brought to him all who were ill with various diseases, those suffering severe pain, the demon-possessed, those having seizures, and the paralyzed, and he healed them. Large crowds from Galilee, the Decapolis, Jerusalem, Judea and the region across the Jordan followed him (Matthew 4:23-25).

After observing His miracles and power, people from all over Israel began to gather around Jesus, and they were quite interested in what He had to teach (see Matt. 5:1-2).

During the Sermon on the Mount, there would have been thousands of people there to hear the message from Jesus' heart.

All those who were there, while they were quite interested in Jesus, did not agree with Him.

As Jesus began to deliver His heart about followers of the kingdom of God, I can hear Him saying: "I have good news, and I have bad news. The good news is that the kingdom of God that you have observed is true. The miracles, healings, and deliverances are real and true. The bad news is that the kingdom of God is not going to come to and flow through who you think."

When Jesus saw the crowds, He went up on the mountain; and after He sat down, His disciples came to Him. He opened His mouth and began to teach them, saying, "Blessed are the poor in spirit, for theirs is the kingdom of heaven. Blessed are those who mourn, for they shall be comforted. Blessed are the gentle, for they shall inherit the earth. Blessed are those who hunger and thirst for righteousness, for they shall be satisfied. Blessed are the merciful, for they shall receive mercy. Blessed are the pure in heart, for they shall see God. Blessed are the peacemakers, for they shall be called sons of God. Blessed are those who have been persecuted for the sake of righteousness, for theirs is the kingdom of heaven" (Matthew 5:1-10 NASB).

Jesus began to bring definition to what followers of the kingdom of God look like and how they respond to the kingdom of God.

You Are Salt

You are the salt of the earth. But if the salt loses its saltiness, how can it be made salty again? It is no longer good for anything, except to be thrown out and trampled by men (Matthew 5:13).

The beatitudes are over, but the Sermon on the Mount continues. As we enter into verse 13, we need to see ourselves still sitting at the feet of Jesus on a hill in Galilee, but something has changed. In the first twelve verses, Jesus is describing the kind of people to whom the kingdom of God comes, the kind of people the power of the kingdom flows through. This is the power that was demonstrated in chapter 4. In verse 13, Jesus is no longer describing kingdom people; He is now talking to them. He is looking them in the eye. Jesus is saying things that are true about them. Today, you need to know that God believes in you!

TODAY, YOU NEED TO KNOW THAT GOD BELIEVES IN YOU!

The "you" are those who are broken, mourning, hungry, and thirsty for righteousness; they are kingdom people. Jesus is making a statement. He is not calling you to act like salt; He is telling you, "You are salt."

Salt and light carried a great connotation in Jesus' day. You need to understand that when Jesus said, "You are the salt of the earth" and "You are the light of the world," He was speaking to the people of that day, but His meaning has not changed. Jesus was, and is, saying to you, "You are the most valuable commodity on the face of the earth."

Jesus' metaphor of salt is significant. We have often spiritualized this text. We salt our food, and it makes us thirsty; therefore, our presence in the world should make people thirsty for God. Salt in a wound stings; therefore, the Church of Jesus Christ needs to confront sin in our culture. We do need to confront sin, and we may make people thirsty for God's presence, but this is not the imagery Jesus is invoking when He tells us that we are the salt of the earth.

There is something more we need to understand about this verse. Salt meant more to people in Jesus' day than it does today. In that culture, salt was something you could not live without. Ancient Greeks used to say, *Except for the sun, there is nothing more important than salt to the existence of mankind.*[1]

Salt was a valuable preservative. They had no refrigeration in Jesus' day, and food was housed in the middle of a stack of salt. It was so important that Roman soldiers would be paid with salt. The actual word for salt is where we get our word for salary. The expression, "This guy is not worth his salt," came from this time in history.[2] Salt was often given as a gift to show appreciation or to acknowledge the depth of intimacy.

In the original context, Jesus was telling people that they were of immeasurable worth and value to the earth. The people listening to Jesus would have understood the metaphor of being compared to salt. They understood that Jesus was calling them a great commodity that had great value on the earth.

God is saying to each of us: "Broken, mourning, hungry, and thirsty people need to know something. You are a valuable commodity. You are more valuable than any other commodity on the earth. Gold and silver are not as valuable as you." God knew of you before the heavens and the earth were created. He anointed you to become the valuable commodity of salt while you were being knit in your mother's womb.

You Are the Light

In Matthew 5:14, Jesus says you are the light of the world. Jesus said, *"...I am the light of the world"* (John 9:5); the light is Christ Himself. In John 8:12, Jesus spoke again to the people and said, *"I am the light of the world. Whoever follows me will never walk in darkness, but will have the light of life."* And Paul said,

> For God, who said, "Let light shine out of darkness," made His light shine in our hearts to give us the light of the knowledge of the glory of God in the face of Christ (2 Corinthians 4:6).

Jesus was the light of the world, and He made us to be light to the world when He returned to heaven. We will draw people with our light, but more importantly, we are literally Christ to the world; we are Jesus with skin on.

JESUS IS SAYING YOU ARE CHRIST IN THE WORLD; YOU ARE JESUS WITH SKIN ON.

Light doesn't mean too much to us; we have it everywhere and at anytime. We simply turn on the light switch, and we have instant light. We tend to take light for granted. Unlike the people of Jesus' day, we don't appreciate light and its presence.

The people of Jesus' day did not have to deal with power and electric companies. Thus, the people of that day understood the importance of light to their society. As Jesus was telling them that they were the light of the world, something clicked within them because they understood that light was such a valuable commodity.

The Stars in the Sky

Always remember this reality. When you consider the stars in the sky, the closest stars are countless light years away, millions of miles from the earth. The stars receive their light from the sun, and the stars are always shining. But when do they shine the most? The stars, while they are constantly shining, shine most powerfully in the darkness! Since you are the light of the world, you shine most powerfully in a dark world. Your very presence in this world is bringing the light of God everywhere you go! Next time you step into your local grocery store, understand that the light of the world just stepped in; God's presence just entered into the room.

The Story of Light, Evil, and Heat

A university professor challenged his students with this question:

"Did God create everything that exists?"

A student bravely replied, "Yes, He did!"

"God created everything?" the professor asked, "So God created all things?"

"Yes sir," the student replied.

The professor responded, "If God created everything, then God created evil since evil exists. According to the principle that our works define who we are, God is evil."

The student became quiet before such an answer.

The professor was quite pleased with himself and boasted to the students that he had proven, once more, that the Christian faith was a myth.

Another student raised his hand and said, "Can I ask you a question, professor?"

"Of course," replied the professor.

The student stood up and asked, "Professor, does cold exist?"

"What kind of question is this? Of course it exists. Have you never been cold?"

The students snickered at the young man's question.

The young man replied, "In fact, sir, cold does not exist."

"According to the laws of physics, what we consider cold is, in reality, the absence of heat. Every body or object is susceptible to study when it has or transmits energy, and heat is what makes a body or matter have or transmit energy. Absolute zero (-460 degrees F) is the total absence of heat; all matter becomes inert and incapable of reaction at that temperature. Cold does not exist. We have created this word to describe how we feel if we have no heat."

The student continued, "Professor, does darkness exist?"

The professor responded, "Of course it does."

The student replied, "Once again you are wrong, sir; darkness does not exist either. Darkness is, in reality, the absence of light. Light we can study, but not darkness. In fact, we can use Newton's prism to break white light into many colors and study the various wavelengths of each color. You cannot measure darkness. A simple ray of light can break into a world of darkness and illuminate it. How can you know how dark a certain space is? You measure the amount of light present. Isn't this correct? Darkness is a term used by people to describe what happens when there is no light present."

 ## EVIL IS SIMPLY THE ABSENCE OF GOD.

Finally the young man asked the professor, "Sir, does evil exist?"

Now uncertain, the professor responded, "Of course, as I have already said. We see it every day. It is in the daily example of people's inhumanity to people! It is in the multitude of crime and violence everywhere in the world. These manifestations are nothing else but evil."

To this the student replied, "Evil does not exist, sir, or at least it does not exist unto itself. Evil is simply the absence of God. It is just like darkness and cold, a word that people have created to describe the absence of God. God did not create evil. Evil is not like faith or love that exist just as do light and heat. Evil is the result of what happens when people do not have God's love present in their hearts. It's like the cold that comes when there is no heat or the darkness that comes when there is no light."

God Is Speaking Clearly

You are salt, and you are light. You may have lost your eternal vision, your belief in yourself, and—worst of all—the reality that God believes in you. You have lost the significance of your existence. God has a high opinion of you, and He has decided to move through you to bring heaven to the earth.

Paul tells us that we were created in His image, *"For we are God's handiwork, created in Christ Jesus to do good works, which God prepared in advance for us to do"* (Eph. 2:10). The Greek word for handiwork is *poiema*, from which we get our word *poem*.[3] We are God's poem to the world, the art that displays His grace, His handiwork of love.

Many would say that God's greatest masterpiece is the sunset that paints the evening sky or the millions of stars that twinkle so beautifully each night. Others might point to the majestic mountain ranges or the mighty, rushing rivers. And some might say the flowers that bloom in the spring or the many amazing creatures that populate our planet.

YES, YOU ARE THE GREATEST OF GOD'S MASTERPIECES.

All of those masterpieces are impressive, but none of them are the greatest that God has created. You are the greatest of God's masterpieces. We are His *"handiwork, created in Christ Jesus"* (Eph. 2:10). God declares from the hallways of heaven, "This is My beloved child, in whom I am well pleased and who I am excited to call My own."

The Masterpiece Is a Process

The creation of a masterpiece is usually not the result of some brief, haphazard effort. The *Mona Lisa* required four years for Da Vinci to complete. In fact, X-rays have shown that there are three previous versions of the painting under the one that we are familiar with. Michelangelo took four years to paint the scenes on the ceiling of the Sistine Chapel. Rodin made his first plaster cast of *The Thinker* in 1880, but it wasn't until 1902 that he completed the large-scale bronze cast.

God is creating you into a masterpiece in your soul realm. Like many of the great works of art, you don't become a finished work of art all at once. Paul writes that we were created (past tense), but we are (present tense) God's masterpiece.

The present tense in Greek indicates a continuing action. So literally we are and will continue to become God's masterpiece. As all of us are painfully aware, we don't immediately become everything that God intends for us to be the very moment that He enters into our lives and makes us a new creation. God allows us to go through a process, one that is often painful, so that He can mold us and make us into what He wants us to be. Like a skillful artist, God sometimes completes us with a stroke of His brush, and at other times He chisels away at our lives to get rid of those things that would detract from our beauty. He will chisel away anything that hinders His love getting to us. Paul writes about that process in one of his letters: *"...he who began a good work in you will carry it on to completion until the day of Christ Jesus"* (Phil. 1:6). God loves to stretch His followers so that we can contain more of Him.

You are a masterpiece of art; you were anointed from your conception. When God first thought of you, He looked at you with pleasure and anticipation, and He believes in you now.

> *I know your deeds. See, I have placed before you an open door that no one can shut. I know that you have little strength, yet you have kept my word and have not denied my name* (Revelation 3:8).

God's heart for you is well-spoken in these verses. God tells us that He has put an open door before us because we have little power; I would add that we haven't seen anything yet!

> *I will make those who are of the synagogue of Satan, who claim to be Jews though they are not, but are liars—I will make them*

come and fall down at your feet and acknowledge that I have loved you (Revelation 3:9).

Your heavenly Father, through the Scriptures, says this to you: "Behold, I am going to give you victory. I believe in you, and I love you simply because you are My creation. You who are kingdom people—who are broken and dependent upon Me, who mourn, who are willing to be real, who hunger and thirst for My righteousness—you need to know that you are the salt of the earth, and you are the light of the world." We all need to know that God, our Creator, who does all things perfect, believes in us!

I BELIEVE IN YOU, AND I LOVE YOU SIMPLY BECAUSE YOU ARE MY CREATION.

You, my friend, are the light of the world. Wherever and whenever you show up, the light of God is there, and evil is dispelled because the power, salt, and light of God is now there! God really does believe in you.

Summary Questions

1. Describe what is unique about the dove's eyes (see page 209).

_____

_____

_____

_____

_____

_____

2. What does it mean to you when Jesus declares in Song of Solomon 1:15 that you have dove's eyes? (See page 209.)

_____

_____

_____

_____

_____

3. What is God's eternal message to each of us? (See page 209.)

_____

_____

_____

_____

_____

4. Read Philippians 3:20 in the NKJV, and see page 214. Where is your citizenship *now?*

_____

_____

_____

_____

_____

5. Read Ephesians 2:6 in the NASB. Spiritually, where are you seated *now?* How does this reality make you want to operate in this life?

_____

_____

_____

_____

_____

_____

6. Write about what it feels like to know God believes in you. (See pages 214-215.)

_____

_____

_____

_____

_____

_____

_____

_____

7. Read Matthew 5:13 in the NIV. Write about the value ascribed to salt in the time when Jesus made His statement in Matthew 5:13 and what this means for you. (See pages 215-217.)

_____

_____

_____

_____

_____

8. Read Matthew 5:14; John 8:12; John 9:5; and Second Corinthians 4:6 in the NIV. Jesus says you are the light of the world and declares He is the light of the world. Reckoning the value of light as a commodity in Jesus' day, describe what it means to you to be the light of the world (see pages 217-218).

_____

_____

_____

_____

_____

_____

9. Evil is simply the absence of _____. Darkness is the absence of _____ (see page 220).

10. You are a masterpiece in progress! (See pages 221-222.) Fill in the blank: "He who began a good work in you will carry it on to _____ until the day of Christ Jesus" (Phil. 1:6).

Endnotes

1. "Worth One's Salt," *The Phrase Finder,* http://www.phrases.org.uk/meanings/worth-ones-salt.html (accessed February 17, 2012).

2. Ibid.

3. Thayer and Smith, *The KJV New Testament Greek Lexicon,* s.v. "Poema" (#4161); BibleStudyTools.com; http://www.biblestudytools.com/lexicons/greek/kjv/poiema.html (accessed February 17, 2012).

Chapter 14

God Says You Have All Authority

We not only have eternal protection from the enemy of God, but we have full and complete authority over him.

I n this final chapter, we will focus in on the reality that the bridal paradigm message is shouting out that each believer as the Bride of Christ has an inheritance and where that authority is ignited and released.

God gave humans the ability to make choices. This is a great act of devotion toward the human race. God is looking for voluntary lovers and followers who will operate in the dominion that God has given them. Dominion simply means we have all authority. What power and glory was given to humanity! Our greatest source of power and authority rests on the shoulders of intercession.

Authority and Power Have Not Changed

As the Bride of Christ, we must embrace the spirit of intercession through Jesus, the Chief Intercessor. Jesus' job description in heaven is that of the premier intercessor. It could be said that this is what Jesus lives for. Up to this point in history, the Bride of Christ has seldom stepped into her role as an intercessor. As the Bride of Christ, we need to know that all of our authority and protection rests on the shoulders of our intercession. This is why God is raising up houses of prayer throughout the earth.

The first century Church apostles ignited a devotion to *prayer* and the *Word of God* (see Acts 2:42; 6:4). If the Church apostles spent a normal eight-hour day in ministry, and they only moved in two things, prayer and ministry of the Word, then they spent four hours per day in prayer. It is amazing that we currently see little authority and power over the enemy. The difference between the Church of today and the early Church is one thing: prayer! Prayer was the fuel that catapulted Peter from the upper room to preaching so that three thousand people received salvation (see Acts 1:14; 2:41-42).

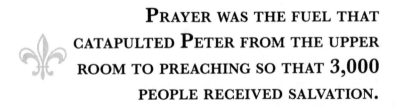

PRAYER WAS THE FUEL THAT CATAPULTED PETER FROM THE UPPER ROOM TO PREACHING SO THAT 3,000 PEOPLE RECEIVED SALVATION.

Today we are less concerned about church leadership having a deep devotion to God's Word and intercession and more concerned that church leaders are organized, are counselors, and are individuals with soul-winning charm and personalities that draw people to the church.

Jesus Speaks of Night-and-Day Prayer

In Luke 18, Jesus provokes His disciples by challenging their traditions. He asks, *"...When the Son of Man comes, will He find faith on the earth?"* (Luke 18:8). His question is a warning to Christians who would limit the power of God at the end of the age. Jesus is calling us to resist our powerless traditions; He is asking us individually, *"Will I find faith in you?"*

Jesus clearly states in Luke 18 that night-and-day prayer is the fuel that will drive His justice. Jesus deliberately equates faith with night-and-day prayer. To Jesus, they are inseparable. Jesus did not ask, *"Will I find programs implemented? Will you be in board meetings? Will I find your doctrine correct?"* What we believe is quite important, but it never rises above the spirit of intercession.

If we are going to step into the authority that we *have been* given, then we can expect the supernatural move of God to be imparted on our behalf as we encounter night-and-day prayer and, in particular, when we do not lose heart (see Luke 18:1).

Jesus demonstrates the importance of our authority through intercession by giving a parable about a widow who petitioned a judge who had no respect for people, much less God (see Luke 18:1-8). Because she continued to cry out, the judge gave her the legal protection that was legally hers. God gives us legal right to wear Him out (see Luke 18:5). Jesus concluded by saying,

> And the Lord said, *"Listen to what the unjust judge says. And will not God bring about justice for his chosen ones, who cry out to him day and night? Will he keep putting them off? I tell you, he will see that they get justice, and quickly...* (Luke 18:6-8).

I Must Have More of God

It is significant that Jesus compared His elect to a widow harassed by an enemy. The widow has legitimate reasons to quit, but instead, she prevails. She refuses to remove herself from her highest potential simply because of her lowly state. She makes no apologies for her lack of finances, wisdom, or charisma. Giving herself no reason to fail, she boldly states her case before the judge, where she pleads for and receives what is hers: legal protection from her opponent.

Being Desperate Defines Your Authority

How did a common widow gain such authority? We can imagine that there must have been a time when, under the relentless pressure of her adversary, she became desperate, and desperation worked to her advantage. Desperation is God's mallet. It demolishes the stronghold of fear and shatters the chains of our excuses. When our desperation for God exceeds our fears, the kingdom of God advances.

Your desperation for God provides the legal protection that the widow pleaded for. You are the widow who has now received all power and authority to defeat the enemy of God. As we are relentless through intercession, we will see the justice of God released on our behalf into all the earth! As we persevere, let us keep praying and never settle for failure. For this is what the Bride of Christ does. She stays on the wall of intercession, moving in her authority, and prays for justice!

Focus Your Authority

Through the spirit of intercession and boldness, the Church is beginning to take our position seriously as we stand against the enemy of God. The problem, historically, has been where we place our focus. When we place our time, energy, and spiritual resources on the devil instead of on the majesty and beauty of God, we have lost our power and authority. We have to admire the admonition that James gives us.

> *Submit yourselves, then, to God. Resist the devil, and he will flee from you. Come near to God and he will come near to you...* (James 4:7-8).

The first thing that we are commanded to do is to submit to God. Remember the word *submit* means to agree with God. The way we resist the devil is by coming near to God. As we focus on the power and beauty of God, remember that He will, from time to time, prompt us to speak directly to the enemy. But, this is not our focus or concentration. All of our protection and authority rests on the shoulders of intercession and agreement with Jesus as we draw near to God and focus on His nature and character.

Given Protection and Authority

When Christ died on the cross, heaven made a declaration of truth. The debt that we owed was canceled, and we were brought from death into life. Along with our sins being forgiven, this decree also declared and guaranteed protection for the Bride of Christ. This eternal shield provides guaranteed protection from the enemy of God. This means that we not only have eternal protection *from* the enemy of God, but that we also have complete and full authority *over* him.

> *When you were dead in your sins and in the uncircumcision of your flesh God made you alive with Christ. He forgave us all our sins, having canceled the charge of our legal indebtedness, which stood against us and condemned us; he has taken it away, nailing it to the cross.* **And having disarmed the powers and authorities, he made a public spectacle of them, triumphing over them by the cross** (Colossians 2:13-15).

We, as believers and followers of God, stand on Jesus' ceiling. The things that Jesus contended to bring from heaven to earth have become the foundation that we stand upon. Jesus' death on the cross and His ascension from the dead have given us the ability to stand on His power and authority.

WE, AS BELIEVERS AND FOLLOWERS OF GOD, STAND ON JESUS' CEILING.

We have been given ultimate authority to engage in spiritual warfare against the enemy of God. Our greatest and most powerful source of spiritual warfare is declaring God's Word of truth against all evil and ushering in God's justice to the earth through intercession.

Faith of Reality

The faith of reality is the essence of who we are. This faith holds things as true, even if they appear as contrary evidence to what we see. Jesus said that mustard seed faith could move mountains.

> *And He said to them, "Because of the littleness of your faith; for truly I say to you, if you have faith the size of a mustard seed, you will say to this mountain, "Move from here to there," and it will move; and nothing will be impossible to you* (Matthew 17:20 NASB).

This practice of faith is based on the power of God and the evidence of the things that He has done in the past. When you begin to reason with your Kingdom mind, then your attitude is shifted toward His heart and His miracles. You must begin to put the revelation that God has given you into practice. This means the faith that we experience must shape the way we think and, therefore, the way we live and function.

THE FAITH THAT WE EXPERIENCE MUST SHAPE THE WAY WE THINK.

In *The Supernatural Power of a Transformed Mind*, Bill Johnson discusses from Mark 6:30-44 how we need to learn from miracles and the influence miracles can have on our identity in God.[1] Bill is an amazing author, and his understanding into this passage is full of the Spirit and brilliant. I must add a few of my own thoughts on this passage. This miracle story illustrates the need to learn as Bill mentions, from each miracle, but beautifully illustrates our need to remember who we are.

Here is the story.

The apostles gathered around Jesus and reported to him all they had done and taught. Then, because so many people were coming and going that they did not even have a chance to eat, he said to them, "Come with me by yourselves to a quiet place and get some rest." So they went away by themselves in a boat to a solitary place. But many who saw them leaving recognized them and ran on foot from all the towns and got there ahead of them. When Jesus landed and saw a large crowd, he had compassion on them, because they were like sheep without a shepherd. So he began teaching them many things.

By this time it was late in the day, so his disciples came to him. "This is a remote place," they said, "and it's already very late. Send the people away so that they can go to the surrounding countryside and villages and buy themselves something to eat."

But he answered, "You give them something to eat."

They said to him, "That would take more than half a year's wages! Are we to go and spend that much on bread and give it to them to eat?"

"How many loaves do you have?" he asked. "Go and see."

When they found out, they said, "Five—and two fish."

Then Jesus directed them to have all the people sit down in groups on the green grass. So they sat down in groups of hundreds and fifties. Taking the five loaves and the two fish and looking up to heaven, he gave thanks and broke the loaves. Then he gave them to his disciples to distribute to the people. He also divided the two fish among them all. They all ate and were satisfied, and the disciples picked up twelve basketfuls of broken pieces of bread and fish. The number of the men who had eaten was five thousand (Mark 6:30-44).

The disciples participated in the incredible miracle of a great increase of food at the feeding of the five thousand. This miracle took place in their hands, not in Jesus' hands. Jesus didn't say, "Appear," and suddenly a massive amount of food appeared! He took the small portions and placed it in the hands of the disciples and, as they gave it away, it multiplied. Jesus simply blessed the food, but the disciples carried out the miracle!

Suffice it to say that the disciples were astounded at the miracle of food multiplying, but they were equally astonished that the miracle occurred through their hands, not Jesus' hands. I believe that, at that moment, they had a spiritual epiphany. It hit them like a ton of bricks that—out of their obedience and agreement with Jesus—the power of God was and is real. They knew at that moment who God was and who they were!

Later that day, Jesus told them to sail over to the other side of the Sea of Galilee in their boat, and Jesus went to a mountainside to pray. In the Spirit, Jesus saw His disciples straining to row their boat because of a storm. They were almost ready to lose their lives.

He saw the disciples straining at the oars, because the wind was against them. Shortly before dawn he went out to them, walking on the lake. He was about to pass by them, but when they saw him walking on the lake, they thought he was a ghost. They cried out, because they all saw him and were terrified. Immediately he spoke to them and said, "Take courage! It is I, don't be afraid." Then he climbed into the boat with them, and the wind died down. They were completely amazed, for they had not understood about the loaves; their hearts were hardened (Mark 6:48-52).

Amazingly, they had not remembered the miracle that had taken place through them earlier that day with the loaves and fishes.

The Influence of Remembering

They had completely agreed with and obeyed Jesus when handing out the miracle of fishes and loaves, yet the disciples panicked when they saw what they perceived as a ghost walking on the water. Because they did not remember the results of the previous miracle (feeding the five thousand), they had no solution for the storm that presented itself when Jesus was not in the boat! Jesus calls us to remember who we are, whether He is in the boat with us or not! Jesus had said previously, "You feed them."

Jesus was not going to do the miracle for them. Their obedience caused the food to multiply. Remembering who we are will produce obedience, and that obedience will deliver the kingdom of God. Our mind is heavily influenced by what we agree with. When Jesus spoke in Mark 8:15, *"Be careful...Watch out for the yeast of the Pharisees and that of Herod,"* Jesus was reminding them and us about the influences of the mind. In Mark 8:18-21, Jesus tells the disciples,

> *"Do you have eyes but fail to see, and ears but fail to hear?* **And don't you remember?** *When I broke the five loaves for the five thousand, how many basketfuls of pieces did you pick up?"*

> *"Twelve," they replied.*

> *"And when I broke the seven loaves for the four thousand, how many basketfuls of pieces did you pick up?"*

> *They answered, "Seven."*

> *He said to them,* **"Do you still not understand?"**

Jesus is calling each of us to understand and remember who He is and who He says we are.

As we endeavor to move into the kingdom and experience His power, favor, and miracles, these influences affect our minds. In order for us to see into the unseen world of God, we will have to understand and remember who God says we are. God has each of us on a process of renewing our minds with His truth. This process is called transformation of the mind (see Rom. 12:2). He is giving us right thinking and right beliefs!

You Have Dominion, Now Pray and Go!

Like you, I was created for His great pleasure. The bridal paradigm message communicates that my Heavenly Father created me to be in His presence, completely fascinated and consumed by Him. You too were created and established for this reason. All of the longings we contain will be fully realized when we see Him in His glory.

ALL OF THE LONGINGS WE CONTAIN WILL BE FULLY REALIZED WHEN WE SEE HIM IN HIS GLORY.

We will all know Him and understand all things, and yet we will gaze on His glorious face with an ever increasing and non-ceasing wonder of His infinite grace and glory.

The Bridegroom message is a call to active intimacy with God. The bridal paradigm message speaks of God's invitation for us to experience the deep things of His emotion-filled heart. To enjoy active intimacy with Jesus includes feeling His heart for us. The bridal message speaks of experiencing Jesus' emotions.

Hopefully, now you may know more of who you are as Christ's beloved Bride. God has created you and given you life to re-establish all dominion and authority on the earth by demonstrating love, miracles, signs, and wonders. You were created for His plea-sure and to bring heaven to the earth. Since you have been given His authority, you move in the power and love of heaven. In the name of Jesus Christ, all authority is now yours, so step into the truth and move into your destiny. And always *remember who you are!*

Summary Questions

1. As members of the Bride of Christ, where does our authority begin? (See page 227.)

_____

_____

_____

_____

_____

_____

_____

2. _____ means you have all authority (see page 227).

3. _____ is our greatest source of power and author-ity (see pages 227-228).

4. Read Luke 18:1-8 in the NASB and fill in the blanks. "...Pray and do not lose _____. ...Will not God bring _____ for His elect who cry out _____ and _____? ...When the Son of Man comes will He find _____ on the earth?"

5. Why is it important that we pray and "not lose heart"?

_____

_____

_____

_____

_____

_____

6. How does desperation define your authority? (See page 230.)

_____

_____

_____

_____

7. What happens when you focus your authority? (See page 230-231.)

_____

_____

_____

_____

_____

8. Why do we have eternal protection from the enemy, and what does this mean to us? (See page 231-232.)

_____

_____

_____

_____

_____

Endnote

1. Bill Johnson, *The Supernatural Power of a Transformed Mind* (Shippensburg, PA: Destiny Image, 2005).

Gaining Revelation Through Meditation

Use these tools to help you meditate on Scripture in order to understand who God says you are to Him! Your burning desire for more of God will be increased as you meditate. Use the verses listed on pages 179-182. Stay on one passage for a while. Remember, the goal is not to finish, but to be with Him!

- *Read the passage of Scripture* ten times. Read it slowly and literally.

- *Write out the passage of Scripture* ten times. (If you are using a computer, it is no fair using "control copy, control paste.")

- *Say the passage of Scripture.* Say it with passion and zeal. Say it with your own words. Love language will begin to be formed. Say it until you get it.

- *Sing the passage of Scripture* (for a while).

- *Pray the passage of Scripture over yourself.* Ask God to give you revelation into who you are to Him.

Answer Key

NOTE: This answer key has answers for the fill-in-the-blank questions. The rest of the answers can be searched out in the text of *Remember Who You Are* and the Bible.

Chapter 1: The True Nature of God

7. mourn, comforted

9. a. loved, you, b. world, loved them, loved

Chapter 2: Understanding the Bridal Paradigm

1. bridal paradigm, intercessory worship

2. a. shame, b. fear, c. doubt, d. insecurity

5. a. the body of Christ, b. the sons of God, c. the Bride

8. filled with tender mercy, thrilled and happy heart, fiery affections, zealous, possesses indescribable beauty

9. purpose, living *(and)* existing

Chapter 3: Is There Spiritual Abuse?

2. false

Chapter 4: God's Grace Is Not Difficult

3. spirit, flesh

Chapter 5: Humanity's Deepest Issue

1. death

3. soul, body

4. from God

7. living sacrifice, holy, pleasing

15. mind, will, emotions

Chapter 6: God Makes a Promise

8. a. love, b. joy, c. peace, d. forbearance, e. kindness, f. goodness, g. faithfulness, h. gentleness, and i. self-control

10. a. spirit, b. soul, c. flesh

12. a. know, b. consider (or count), c. present (or yield)

Chapter 7: The Flesh and the Soul

3. natural, supernatural

5. old, sin, died, free from sin

Chapter 8: What Shall We Say, Then?

1. truth, truth, lies

Chapter 9: Do You Think the Law Is Good?

4. grace

5. sin, Commandment, Law, dead

7. created

Chapter 10: Is There a Battle?

No fill-in-the-blanks

Chapter 11: The Cycles

2. God, shame

3. manipulate, control

10. Yes

19. truth, transformation

Chapter 12: God Gives Tools

2. meditate, obey

3. be with Him

4. Supernatural revelation

Chapter 13: God Believes in You

9. God, light

Chapter 14: God Says You Have All Authority

2. Dominion

3. Intercession

4. heart, justice, day, night, faith

About Ken Winton

Ken Winton is the Director of The Prayer House in Chico, California. His desire is to help the body of Christ grow in the bridal paradigm reality. If there is anything Ken can do to assist you, your church, or your house of prayer, please do not hesitate to contact him for speaking engagements, trainings, or a consultation on the phone.

Contact Ken at:

www.kenwinton.org

www.theprayerhouse.com

ken@theprayerhouse.com

IN THE RIGHT HANDS, THIS BOOK WILL CHANGE LIVES!

Most of the people who need this message will not be looking for this book. To change their lives, you need to put a copy of this book in their hands.

> *But others (seeds) fell into good ground, and brought forth fruit, some a hundred-fold, some sixty-fold, some thirty-fold* (Matthew 13:8).

Our ministry is constantly seeking methods to find the good ground, the people who need this anointed message to change their lives. Will you help us reach these people?

> *Remember this—a farmer who plants only a few seeds will get a small crop. But the one who plants generously will get a generous crop* (2 Corinthians 9:6).

EXTEND THIS MINISTRY BY SOWING
3 BOOKS, 5 BOOKS, 10 BOOKS, OR MORE TODAY,
AND BECOME A LIFE CHANGER!

Thank you,

Don Nori Sr., Founder
Destiny Image
Since 1982